MW01115796

Hold The Line

A Call for Christian Conviction in a Culture of Conformity

Erik Reed

kjmin.org

Copyright © 2022 Knowing Jesus Ministries

All rights reserved. No part of this publication may be reproduced, stored in a retrieval system, or transmitted in any form by any means, electronic, mechanical, photocopy, recording, or otherwise, without the prior permission of Knowing Jesus Ministries, except as provided for by USA copyright law.

Cover design: The A Group

Cover image: The A Group

First printing: 2022

Printed in the United States of America

Unless otherwise indicated, Scripture quotations are from the ESV Bible (The Holy Bible, English Standard Version), copyright 2001 by Crossway, a publishing ministry of Good News Publishers. Used by permission. All rights reserved.

All emphases in Scripture quotations have been added by the author.

ISBN: 9798811365180

To my brothers and sisters at The Journey Church, who make pastoring a joy. I'm thankful for your commitment to the Bible, your love for Christ, and your willingness to stand firm in a world where many professing Christians are conforming to the culture. May we never waver as we strive to keep showing Jesus as incomparably glorious.

CONTENTS

ENDORSEMENTS

"To stay faithful to Christ, today's Christian must be keenly aware of what time it is. Erik Reed does, which is why I'm happy to recommend this volume as a critical guide to navigating the difficult terrain of today's culture wars."

- **Andrew Walker**
Associate Professor of Christian Ethics, The Southern Baptist Theological Seminary; Fellow, The Ethics and Public Policy Center.

"We are truly living the days of 2 Timothy 4, when many would rather find teachers who conform to their own desires than to sound doctrine. As hostility towards the teachings of Jesus increases, so does the opportunity among His followers to demonstrate genuine discipleship, the kind that demands nothing less than the totality of one's self. Erik confronts us with Jesus' most challenging commands and reminds us that the call to discipleship is a call to die to ourselves, to resist the ease of conformity, and to fear God alone. In a world of compromise, we must hold the line. "

- **Katie J. McCoy**
Director of Women's Ministry, Texas Baptists Center for Church Health.

"In this much-needed book, Reed deftly demonstrates that the modern American church has spent far too much time trying to remake Christ in the image of the culture, rather than letting Christ remake us. This eminently practical guide offers both reasons and strategies for fighting worldly drift and contending for the faith in a society that increasingly finds biblical principles not just offensive, but alien. More than a warning, *Hold the Line* presents a challenge to believers not to lose their souls for the sake of pleasing men."

- **Megan Basham**

Claremont Fellow, Culture Reporter for *Daily Wire*, *Morning Wire* podcast.

"In an age of confusion and compromise, we need pastors who understand the times, recognize where the pressure is coming from, and speak and act with courage, clarity, and compassion. Erik Reed is one such pastor, and I'm grateful he's written this little book. May it help you to heed the biblical call to stand firm in the evil day."

- **Dr. Joe Rigney**

President of Bethlehem College & Seminary, author of *More Than a Battle: How to Experience Victory, Freedom, and Healing from Lust*

"Peace if possible. Truth at all costs."

— Martin Luther

Introduction:

THE ROOSTER'S CROW

The evening took a turn from anything that Peter and the disciples expected. It shouldn't have been a surprise when soldiers showed up to arrest Jesus. He predicted this was coming. But now their master was gone.

They followed Jesus for three years. Their eyes experienced some of the most incredible things ever witnessed. They watched as Jesus spoke to violent winds and waves, and they obeyed Him. At the home of Mary and Martha, they watched Jesus speak into the tomb where Lazarus lay dead for four days. Lazarus then emerged alive at Jesus' command to come forth. They experienced healings, demons cast into a herd of pigs, water turned into wine, and Jesus walking on water. In addition, they listened to sermon after sermon, enjoyed dinner conversations, had chats as they walked down the road, and attended numerous gatherings in the synagogues as Jesus opened the

Scriptures. The disciples had never heard someone teach with such authority and wisdom. Peter confessed by the insight God gave him that Jesus was the Christ, the Son of the Living God (Matthew 16:16).

Yet the authorities now had Jesus in their possession. It appeared the full power of the Roman Empire and Jewish Sanhedrin might fall on His head. And so the natural question had to be considered: if it fell on His head, would it also fall on their heads?

Peter followed the mob as they whisked Jesus away from the Mount of Olives and into the city. He kept enough distance to see what was happening, while also staying out of the middle of it to remain an anonymous onlooker. The dark veil of night was the fitting cover for the craven and unlawful actions of the religious leaders and their phony prosecution of the Son of God.

Then someone in the crowd spotted Peter. She said to him, "You also were with the Nazarene, Jesus." Peter denied it. He insisted he didn't know what she was talking about. A rooster crowed aloud. Soon Peter was seen a second time. And a servant girl addressed the bystanders, "This man is one of them." Her reference was to Peter, but he again denied it to everyone.

The arrest of Jesus must have been a source of some interest because people lingered to see what would happen. Time passed after Peter's encounter with the servant girl. But bystanders, who heard her claim Peter was with Jesus, eventually spotted him again. They said, "Certainly you are one of them, for you are a Galilean." This led Peter to give his most forceful, desperate reply. He invoked a curse on himself and swore, "I do not know this man of whom you speak." The rooster crowed a second time. That's when Peter remembered what Jesus had told him earlier.

He broke down in tears.

Earlier that evening, Jesus told the disciples his betrayal was at hand. He shocked His friends by saying they were all going to reject Him. Peter, always the most vocal and aggressive of the bunch, refused to believe Jesus. He exclaimed that "Even though they all fall away, I will not." In his mind, there was no way he would deny Jesus. He was ready to go to his death if necessary for his Lord. But Jesus told him that before the evening was over, and the rooster crowed twice, Peter would not only deny Jesus once, but three times. There in the courtyard, after his third denial, and the rooster's second crow, Peter remembered. Jesus was right.

How could this happen? The steely-eyed disciple who was quick to bow his chest and jump into the mix couldn't cower. There was no way he would deny his Savior, right? He was the first to acknowledge Jesus was the Christ, the Son of the Living God! Peter even drew his sword when the soldiers came to arrest Jesus—and used it! He was ready to fight everyone (Luke 22:50). So why was he stumbling now? What happened?

The piercing stares of the bystanders blunted his courage. That which threatened his allegiance to Jesus was clear. In this moment, Peter's best-case scenario was personal rejection and a loss of reputation. Worst case? His life was in danger. Suddenly, the one who believed he could never walk away now did. He buckled under the pressure of the opposing crowds. Rather than stand alone, in desperation Peter sought to conform.

CLEAR & PRESENT DANGER

Everyone reading this runs the same risk as Peter. We can all fall prey to this trap. We can easily be overconfident in our ability to withstand the onslaught of cultural pressure to conform to beliefs and practices others deem acceptable. The temptation to blend in, or even deny belonging to Christ, is becoming more and more present in the life of everyday Christians. At work, in school, and on social media, the pull and tug to fit in, and not stand out, is real. Anyone who believes they are exempt from this temptation is fooling themselves. In the Western world, dominated by post-Christian nations, we will face opposition for belonging to Christ and following His Word for the rest of our lives. Each passing day makes holding the line more difficult.

A World War I pamphlet from 1916 provides written instructions for platoon commanders on taking

over a trench. Most of the combat of that war unfold-
ed in trenches that stretched across hundreds of miles.
The goal was to hold those lines and not to let the enemy run you out or take it over. The pamphlet states
the purpose of the soldiers and provides two questions of assessment for each person to answer. It
reads:

"I AM HERE FOR TWO PURPOSES: TO
HOLD THIS LINE UNDER ALL CIRCUM-
STANCES, AND TO DO AS MUCH DAMAGE AS
POSSIBLE TO THE ENEMY. AM I DOING ALL I
CAN TO MAKE THIS LINE AS STRONG AS
POSSIBLE? AM I AS OFFENSIVE AS I MIGHT
BE WITH ORGANIZED SNIPERS, SNIPER-
SCOPES, RIFLE GRENADES, CATAPULTS, ETC.,
AND PATROLS?"

This pamphlet is a guide for platoon commanders
in war, but I cannot help thinking the instructions have
something to say to Christians about the task we have
in our current day. We live in a world of fast-paced
change. A massive shift has occurred in how people
understand truth and ethics. The Christian foundations
beneath many of society's laws, traditions, and morals
have eroded.

MY PRAYER FOR YOU
For a long time, the church talked about winning

the culture. The reality is we lost. Our culture is God-denying, Christ-minimizing, and self-ruled. God can bring sweeping changes as He did in great revivals throughout history. The arm of the LORD is not shortened (Isaiah 59:1). He can do anything He pleases (Psalm 115:3). However, if He decides to turn the culture around, it will happen because of His power—not ours. What we can do, and indeed must do, is hold the line. That means we hold fast to the essential truths of the Christian faith and commit ourselves to following Jesus no matter how fiercely the cultural winds push against us.

We must hold this line under all circumstances. In the heat of battle, we don't retreat from the trenches. We hope to inflict as much damage as possible on our enemy, Satan, and work to stop the advance of those who do his bidding. We must make the line as strong as possible by teaching Christians the truth of God's Word and training them to live as disciples. Our offensive weapons are evangelism, missions, apologetics, and engagement in the public square.

This book aims to help Christians hold the line of faith in a culture of conformity. The pressure to fold and bend the knee to this world is not going away. Instead of merely lamenting the situation—though we should lament what our culture celebrates and embraces as truth—we must engage in the fight. Holding the line is not a passive endeavor. It is action-oriented.

If you are a new Christian, looking to grow in your

faith and strengthen your understanding of what it means to follow Christ in the world, my prayer is that this book will outline for you what it takes to stay faithful amidst cultural pressure.

For the longtime Christian discouraged by what you see in the world, who feels like disengaging and retreating from the front lines, my prayer is that you would stay. The church needs you in this crucial hour. Younger believers need your wisdom, knowledge, and love. It is vital to recognize that God has purposed when and where we would live in history (Acts 17:26). We are here for such a time as this (Esther 4:14).

For the individual who once called themselves a Christian, but has walked away, or perhaps you still call yourself a Christian, but you've changed many of your beliefs to better fit the cultural moment we live in, my prayer is for you to read this with a prayerful posture. Ask God to reveal the truth to you about His Word and what it teaches, and what He expects of those who say they belong to Him. Remember, Jesus asks why we would call Him "Lord, Lord" but not do what He commands (Luke 6:46). The good news for you is that Jesus eventually restored Peter as a disciple, despite his three denials (John 21:15-17). Peter later confesses his love for Jesus—three times. And from then on, Peter would live his life holding the line. In fact, he would go to his death on a cross, crucified upside down, in Rome in 64 AD. Why? Because he refused to deny his Savior, Jesus. You can return to Christ too.

Confess your love for Him and live for Him.

For everyone reading this, may Jesus show you his glory and grace. May the truth of God's Word convict your hearts, so that a courage rises to live for Him in a world that will not applaud you for doing it. May you hold the line.

1

THE EVER-LURKING THREAT

One of the greatest threats to Christians in America today is our tendency to conform our beliefs and morals to align with the culture. Everyone is conforming to something. For Christians, we want to conform more and more to Christ. We want our ideas, our words, and our actions to be holy and godly. However, the temptation Christians face is to forsake conforming to the image of Jesus and to adopt the ways of this world.

I have a friend who went from being a Bible-believing and Bible-obeying Christian to someone who threw off all restraints and adopted the prevailing ideas of our culture. She went from someone with a biblical view of sexuality and marriage to someone who denied Scripture's teaching on the subject and married another woman. We had many conversations along the way, and each time I faced the charge of being judgmental and unloving to her. I was "injuring" her by my disagreement, even though my tone was kind. I never once said anything mean, nor raised my voice, but her conclusion about my disagreement was that I was homophobic and unlike Christ. This was hard to hear from someone my family loved, and still loves. No one wants to be viewed that way. But here I was, accused of being a homophobic bigot.

SCARY TRENDS

The last several decades reveal a decline in Christian convictions on what were once broadly-held orthodox beliefs. Belief that the Bible is the inspired, inerrant, and authoritative Word of God is on the decline. According to Gallup, only 24% of Americans believe the Bible is the literal Word of God, down significantly from prior decades.[1] Key doctrines like the Exclusivity of Jesus and the Divinity of Jesus are no longer undisputed tenets of the Christian faith. Studies show a consistent decline in theological understanding and convictions among professing Christians in America.

There are also startling statistics pertaining to young adults. Two-thirds of professing Christians walk away from the church and any commitment to Christ within two years of graduating high school. Think about that. In a youth group of one hundred students,

---

[1] https://news.gallup.com/poll/210704/record-few-americans-believe-bible-literal-word-god.aspx

statistics say sixty-six of them are going to walk away from biblical Christianity within two years of graduation.

This is staggering. It should stun us. Or perhaps more accurately, it should terrify us. Most of these professing believers grew up in Christian homes and attended church for years. How can that many people fall away? How can those Christians no longer have anything to do with Christ?

Couple these statistics with the shifting beliefs of those who continue in the faith and profess to be Christians, and you get a snapshot of a church in crisis. America's churches have big troubles. There seems to be a greater likelihood for professing Christians to believe what the world says instead of believing what God says. More and more Christians appear to take their theological and moral directions from the culture instead of the Bible.

I WOULD NEVER

Is that you? How do your beliefs line up when compared to the culture and to the Bible? What are you being conformed to: Christ or the culture?

There's a good chance as you read this your inner-lawyer is coming to your defense. "Not me!" "I would never turn away from Jesus." "I won't walk away from the church." "I will not let the world determine what I believe." "The Bible is my authority. Nothing's changing that." Maybe you mean those things. Perhaps you are sincere when you reject the possibility that you could conform to the world. And yet so many do. People's beliefs keep shifting further away from biblical orthodoxy. People's convictions morph into alignment with the culture rather than drifting towards biblical teaching.

We saw what Peter did already when he felt the pressure. The Pharisees in Jesus' day didn't recognize Jesus as the Messiah or His message as being from God. But it wasn't because they lacked intelligence. No, Jesus says their problem was "they loved the glory that comes from man more than the glory that comes from God" (John 12:43). They loved the approval and adoration of the crowds. This filtered everything they heard and witnessed from Jesus. They couldn't accept him because it would cost them their big dealness. It is hard to maintain status and notoriety when following Jesus gains you insults instead of praise.

Jesus says in the beatitudes "Blessed are you when others revile you and persecute you and utter all kinds of evil against you falsely on my account. Rejoice and be glad, for your reward is great in heaven, for so they persecuted the prophets who were before you" (Matthew 5:11-12). Expect others to revile you. Persecution is normative for Christians. Jesus says to rejoice and be glad when these things happen because we have a greater reward in heaven. People persecuted the prophets throughout the Old Testament. This is the plight of the faithful children of God.

Jesus comforts His disciples that are hated by the world by reminding them the world hated Jesus first (John 15:18). The world hates Christians because we are not of this world (John 15:19) and we refuse to join in the rebellion against God and His ways. Following Jesus draws the ire and hatred of the world because the world does not love God. They hate Him. And the hard truth is that because the world hates God, the world will hate us too.

But not everyone can handle being hated by others. Most of us long to be accepted and loved by all. This is what leads people to cave against resistance. Judas betrayed Jesus for thirty pieces of silver and the approval of the Pharisees. He walked with Jesus for three years as a witness to incredible miracles yet chose cheap substitutes over God in the flesh. How is that possible? Who in the world would make such a foolish choice?

Those questions are the subject this book seeks to answer.

DO NOT CONFORM

In his letter to the church in Rome, Paul wrote to the believers,

Do not be conformed to this world, but be transformed by the renewal of your mind, that by testing

you may discern what is the will of God, what is good and acceptable and perfect. — Romans 12:2

Why did Paul need to command the Christians in Rome not to conform? Because it was a real possibility. They faced constant threats against their faith. The culture in Rome then, and the culture in America now, are not far apart. Sexual sin abounded. Corruption infested government, businesses, and the military. The cities reeked of the rot infusing its debased culture. And the culture in Rome permeated all the places they conquered. This helps us understand why each of Paul's letters deal with the sin issues Christians were confronting. Not only were their hearts prone to sin, but the culture they lived in promoted and celebrated it. So, Paul warns them to flee from sin because they cannot remain in that sin and inherit the kingdom of God (1 Corinthians 6:9-20).

Paul exhorts the Roman Christians not to conform to this world. Conforming means to become like, or to take the shape of, something else. The Christians in Rome needed to avoid taking the shape of the surrounding culture. Paul wanted them to pursue holiness and live set apart from the world. Jesus called them to that.

Why did Paul need to tell them not to conform? Because the temptation was real. The possibility was strong. There is an ever-lurking threat every Christian faces, each day, to conform to the world and culture around them. The church today needs to heed Paul's warning afresh. Fellow believer, and blood-bought sinner, do not conform to this world. Live set apart. Flee the temptation to become like our culture today. This is not an exhortation for the super committed Christian to follow. This is what it means to be a Christian. Resisting the temptation to conform to the world is the charge for every disciple of Jesus.

My goal is to help you understand why conformity is so common, and to help you guard yourself against it. To do that, we need a clear understanding of what being a disciple of Jesus actually requires of us. And we turn our attention to that topic in the next chapter.

Discussion Questions

1. What is your initial reaction to the idea that you are actively being conformed to something or someone?

2. In what areas of your life do you see yourself being conformed to Christ?

3. In what areas of your life are you seeing yourself being conformed to the culture, or most susceptible to being conformed?

4. Read John 15:19. What does it look like to be "hated" for our faith in Christ in 21st century America?

2

TERMS AND CONDITIONS

Christians are disciples of Jesus. Plain and simple, that's the meaning. Disciples are those who live to follow the teachings of their Master and Lord. Disciples of Jesus live to follow Him. The Scriptures are our guide for knowing who God is and what He requires from us. Jesus sets the terms and conditions of what it means to follow Him and call ourselves Christians. We don't get to customize our experience and create a tailor-made program for belonging to Him. There is no drag-and-drop feature to create a version of the faith to suit our personal likings.

Most Christians will nod their heads at what I just wrote, but we often neglect and ignore clear teachings that Jesus gives to us. Jesus says some very direct things about what it means to be His disciple. And these things are often missing in our sermons, Bible studies, and personal understanding of what it means to be a Christian.

And he said to all, "If anyone would come after me, let him deny himself and take up his cross daily and follow me. For whoever would save his life will lose it, but whoever loses his life for my sake will save it. For what does it profit a man if he gains the whole world and loses or forfeits himself? For whoever is ashamed of me and of my words, of him will the Son of Man be ashamed when he comes in his glory and the glory of the Father and of the holy angels. — Luke 9:23-26

Jesus sets expectations for anyone who comes after Him. Self-denial is the starting point. We must die to ourselves, our dreams, our wants, our wishes, our will, and our glory. Our lives no longer belong to us. If we try to save our lives and hang on to them for our purposes and glory, attempting to just add a little Jesus to them, we will lose our lives. But if we lay down our lives and surrender all to Jesus, we will save them.

Those are piercing statements. He doesn't mince words. Real disciples no longer view their lives as their own. Everything belongs to Jesus. Our natural reaction, in our flesh, is to protest that the price seems too steep. "Is that really what Jesus is asking for?" "Do I really need to do all that to be a Christian?" Yes. Not because I say so, but because Jesus says so. These are His words.

THE WORTH OF A SOUL

Notice the argument Jesus uses to force us to reckon with those conditions. He says, "For what does it profit a man if he gains the entire world and loses or forfeits himself?" It is a rhetorical question. The answer is "nothing!" You gain nothing if you gain the universe but end up losing yourself or your soul (Mark 8:36). Living a life of luxury, acceptance, and status means nothing if you lose your soul. Jesus is giving us perspective. Who cares if everyone loves you and exalts you for eighty years of life, if in the end you are damned forever? Who cares if nobody ever says a negative word about you, if in the end you lose your soul? What does it profit you if the world sings your praises, if in the end Christ tells you to depart from Him (Matthew 7:23)?

The answers to these questions are simple: no one, nothing, zilch, nada. There is no gain or reward for having everything in this world but spending our eternity in everlasting misery. And Jesus tells us plainly that if we are ashamed of Him in this life, He will be ashamed of us before the Father when He returns in his glory. Take note: if you are afraid of identifying with Jesus because of what it will cost you in social capital, He will not identify with you when you are standing in judgment before Almighty God (Matthew

19

10:32-33).

But what about Peter? Peter denied Jesus and was ashamed to be counted as one of his disciples. Did Jesus deny Peter belonged to Him before the Father when Peter died? No. Because Peter repented and lived the rest of his life for Christ. He confessed his sin of denying Jesus and never did it again. His faith in Christ, and allegiance to him, guided the rest of his days. If we have struggled to identify with Christ because of embarrassment or fear of rejection, we should also confess and repent. Just as Peter did, we should renew our allegiance to Jesus and live our faith out in public, regardless of what it costs us. In Peter's case, it eventually cost his life to proclaim Jesus as Lord throughout the world.

MORE HARD SAYINGS

A few chapters later in Luke's Gospel, we find Jesus once again kicking over a hornet's nest with his teachings.

Now great crowds accompanied him, and he turned and said to them, "If anyone comes to me and does not hate his own father and mother and wife and children and brothers and sisters, yes, and even his own life, he cannot be my disciple. Whoever does not bear his own cross and come after me cannot be my disciple. For which of you, desiring to build a tower, does not first sit down and count the cost, whether he has enough to complete it? Otherwise, when he has laid a foundation and is not able to finish, all who see it begin to mock him, saying, 'This man began to build and was not able to finish.' Or what king, going out to encounter another king in war, will not sit down first and deliberate whether he is able with ten thousand to meet him who comes against him with twenty thousand? And if not, while the other is yet a great way off, he sends a delegation and asks for terms of peace. So therefore, any one of you who does not renounce all that he has cannot be my disciple." — Luke 14:25-33

Notice first that great crowds accompanied Jesus. Anytime you see this in the Gospels, you should brace yourself for what's coming. Your antenna should go up, putting you on high alert that something is about to go down. "Why," you ask? Because when the crowds swelled around Jesus, He tended to say things that ran them off.

When great crowds surrounded Him in John 6, He told everyone they had to eat His flesh and drink His blood. That did the trick. People left. Not only did people leave, but Jesus didn't chase them down begging them to return. He let them walk. When they couldn't grasp what He meant by "eat my flesh and drink my blood," and they decided the teaching was too hard and left, Jesus didn't rush after them to explain it was just a metaphor or an analogy. He let them walk and then asked the twelve disciples, "Are you going to leave too?" (John 6:67).

Far from trying to keep the enormous crowds from leaving Him, Jesus cleared them out with precise words about the true cost of following Him. So when we read in Luke 14 that the crowds are large, it shouldn't surprise us that some of His most shocking words are coming.

HATERS

Jesus said, "If anyone comes to me and does not hate his own father and mother and wife and children and brothers and sisters, yes, and even his own life, he cannot be my disciple." How often have you seen this verse printed on a t-shirt? Do you have any coffee mugs or bumper stickers with this one on it? I imagine nobody has this as their life verse. Read it again.

"Hate."

Jesus challenges us to recognize that being a disciple isn't something we squeeze into the existing hustle and bustle of our lives. He comes first. He's the centerpiece. Every other relationship takes a backseat to Him. He forces re-prioritization.

Think about how offensive this is. Jesus tells people they must hate their own father, mother, wife, and children in order to be His disciple. Was Jesus crazy? Who is going to hate their family to follow Him? Is He really asking that of us? Of course not. He's not telling us to literally hate them. He is God in the flesh, the same God who tells us to honor our father and mother, and to love our wife as Christ loves the church. The invitation isn't to trade loving your close family for hating them, it is to love Jesus to such a degree that every other relationship appears as hate in comparison. It is figurative language, but Jesus is speaking to the root of our allegiance.

So, if you are going to follow Jesus, and obeying Him puts you in conflict with your father or spouse, obeying Jesus wins. Your father loses. Your wife loses. Following Jesus means He is our Lord and Master, and that means our children, parents, and especially ourselves, can't be. We must hate even our own life. We must die to ourselves and our claim to lordship over our lives. That's what disciples do. Jesus calls the shots. His Word trumps every other person's word, including our own.

This is why Jesus says in Luke 12:49-53, "I came to cast fire on the earth, and would that it were already kindled! I have a baptism to be baptized with, and how great is my distress until it is accomplished! Do you think that I have come to give peace on earth? No, I tell you, but rather division. For from now on in one house there will be five divided, three against two and two against three. They will be divided, father against son and son against father, mother against daughter and daughter against mother, mother-in-law against her daughter-in-law and daughter-in-law against mother-in-law."

Notice the language again about division. He says He did not come to give peace on earth. What does this mean? I thought Jesus was the Prince of Peace? He is. But He gives peace to the person who lays down his life to follow Him. He gives peace to the restless heart needing redemption, reconciliation, and rest from their weariness and troubles. His offer of peace does not mean peace with everyone else in the world. There is a reason. His coming will cause turmoil. Allegiance to Jesus produces conflict within families, marriages, and societies. People divide over Jesus. Following Him, and taking up His Word and obeying it, will put us at odds with many people in the world, including those closest to us.

If we don't bear our own cross and come after Jesus, we cannot be His disciples. What does that mean? It means that each of us must reckon with our allegiances and devotions. Each person must come to terms with the cost of discipleship. There are things each person must part with to follow Jesus.

Christians don't add a little Jesus into our lives; we radically reorient everything to Him. Following Jesus may cost you relationships. It can cost you status and popularity. Being His disciple will call you to turn from sin that you may have your identity built around, such as being a ladies' man or being gay. Every person must take up his own cross and follow Jesus if they want to be a disciple. The implication is that unwillingness to take up your cross and follow demonstrates you do not follow Jesus.

Jesus says three different times in the passage the words "cannot be my disciple." We are not accustomed to Jesus excluding anyone. In our culture, we pretend as if Jesus will be whoever you want Him to be, so long as you give Him some sort of devotion or respect. But this text presents us with something different. He reveals that unless you follow Him the way He requires, you cannot be His disciple. Three times, He specifies that reality. Note that and do not dismiss its significance.

DO THE MATH

Jesus finishes these challenging thoughts with two parables. The first is about a man who starts building a structure that he cannot finish because he ran out of resources. He didn't count the cost. He didn't calculate what they needed to get the job done. The result? An unfinished structure, which people walked by and mocked its builder as a fool because he didn't count the cost.

The second parable is of a king who hastily goes out to battle without first determining what sort of opposing armies he's going to meet on the battlefield. When he arrives, he discovers the defeat of his army is inevitable. So, the king must send delegates to sue for peace, to negotiate terms of peace before the battle even begins. The king, in humiliation, surrenders before the fight begins because he didn't calculate before rushing in. He didn't count the cost.

Jesus' point in these parables is that if we are to follow Him and be His disciples, we must count the cost first. He will demand everything from us. Terms and conditions are not flexible. Full devotion and allegiance are the expectation for His disciples. So before signing up to follow, make sure you are ready to hate all in comparison. Be ready to shoulder your cross. Count the cost.

As we saw in Luke 9, Jesus' most compelling justification is that keeping your comfort, popularity, and status are not worth losing your soul over. Who cares if father, mother, wife, and child approve of you if the Living God doesn't? Count the cost of following Jesus. But once you count it, realize the cost of not following Him is far greater.

Do Jesus' words in Luke 9 and Luke 14 sound familiar to you? Is this the typical description of being a Christian you hear in sermons and Sunday school? Is this how most Christians approach following Jesus? Those questions are likely answered with, "No." I doubt many responded with, "We hear this all the time at church. At least challenge us with something new."

For many Christians, these passages sound like a different message than what is often taught in their churches and heard from their preachers. Our culture doesn't perceive Christianity to be about what we just outlined in those passages of Scripture either. Jesus compared following Him to a sword. It will divide people from one another, and if you are not prepared to follow Him with that kind of devotion, you cannot be his disciple.

So why have we lost this message? How did we get to the place where these teachings are almost unrecognizable in the American church? That's the subject we turn to now.

Discussion Questions

1. What does it mean to be a disciple of Jesus?

2. What has being a disciple of Jesus cost you?

3. In what areas of your life are you hanging onto things that are hindering your growth in Christ (e.g., dreams, relationships, activities, or possessions)?

4. Christ offers restoration in Him, just as He restored Peter. Where do you need to repent for areas of your life you've not given to Christ and be restored in Him?

5. Are you seeking out biblical teaching that would challenge you to daily count the cost? Or are you settling for teaching that offers a "comfortable Christianity"? What are some passages in the Bible that can help you discern the teaching you're hearing?

3

LOW-BAR CHRISTIANITY

The seeker-sensitive movement of the 1990s and 2000s was very popular. In some circles, it still is. During that time, many church leaders started looking at the culture in America and thinking about ways the church could respond to that culture to reach people for Jesus. For most, the motives were noble and well-intended. Many just wanted to reach lost people with the gospel. However, the tactics and the strategies developed for doing so set into motion many of the things the church is struggling with today.

The seeker-sensitive movement was built upon the idea that unchurched or lost people didn't go to church because it wasn't a relevant and dynamic experience. People weren't interested in preaching. They wanted help for their marriages, finances, and parenting. Theology wasn't as important as building relationships. Church had to be fun, practical, and relevant—and you needed coffee. The kids needed to leave church excited to return the next week.

These things are not all bad (I love coffee and want children to enjoy church), but the driving principle behind all of it was this: the lost and unchurched are the customer, and we tailor everything to satisfy them. This movement had different manifestations and nuances, but the general approach remained the same. This is not only an unbiblical philosophy of ministry, but it created a harmful theological wake behind it. The gospel became secondary in many of these churches, if it was present at all. Churches and pastors proclaimed and fostered a me-centered universe in which the individual's needs, desires, and wants were most important. God existed to meet our needs, clear our path from troubles, bless our selfish endeavors, and ensure our will prevailed. But above all else, the seeker-sensitive philosophy warned against saying or doing anything that unchurched people found offensive or confrontational.

Living a happy life was the goal, but "happy" was defined by cultural and worldly standards instead of the Bible. Everything else, including God, was a means to attain that end. Being a good person was desirable. But even if you messed up, God forgave you because He is a loving God. As long as you're good more than you are bad, you go to Heaven when you die. And until that Day, anytime you have a problem, just take it to God to resolve. Someone coined the phrase "moralistic therapeutic deism" to describe this movement.

This version of Christianity dominates the American evangelical church and has for decades. It pervades churches everywhere, of all denominations. Many professing Christians hold these sub-biblical beliefs and views, while neglecting what the Bible actually teaches. And there are many preachers of notoriety and acclaim who advance these ideas through their sermons, books, podcasts, and articles. Some professing Christians have never known anything different. They assume this is what it means to be a Christian, and everything around them confirms this belief.

We must recover the biblical understanding of the Christian life. Followers of Jesus must return to Jesus' own words about what it means to belong to Him. Disciples of Jesus must once again take their cues about their faith from Jesus instead of the world.

DESPERATE FOR RESPECTABILITY

Why does this description of Christianity sound more familiar to us than the description in the previous chapter? How did self-denial, submitting to Christ's authority, and embracing suffering become so foreign to our understanding of Christianity?

Notice that Jesus' description of being His disciple in Luke 9 and 14 raises the bar much higher than these modern requirements of being a Christian. Jesus talks about hating parents, spouse, child, and yourself if you're going to follow Him. But pastors and churches today lower the bar in the name of "reaching more people." We preach and proclaim a version of Christianity that makes it sound like Jesus is simply overjoyed we would even choose to sign up to be on His team. We act as if we flatter Jesus because we sometimes wear His jersey. Our self-importance, coupled with a low view of Jesus, leads us to feel we can customize our own version of Christianity because Jesus is just so doggone thrilled we'd follow Him at all.

Friends, this is not so. When the crowds swelled, and following Jesus seemed like the popular thing to do, He preached a crowd-clearing message to run off the pretenders. Jesus isn't interested in our half-hearted devotion. He doesn't want our part-time allegiance. Our Lord is no attention-deprived Savior, desperate for any publicity we might give Him. He is the King of glory. He is worthy of all our worship and devotion, but in need of none of it.

So how did we get here? How did we replace the message of surrendered allegiance to all Jesus' commands to thinking the occasional tip of the cap satisfies Him? The answer parallels the church lowering the bar in hopes of reaching more people. But it goes even further than moralistic therapeutic deism. Christian preaching in America today is often marked by a need for cultural respectability. That's the bottom line. We've altered the Bible's message about following Jesus to make Christianity more acceptable to people. We want the world to like us.

Instead of the high standard of renouncing our

right to self-directed lives, we've proclaimed and projected a version of Christianity that lets people customize their own personal experience with Jesus. We lowered the bar so low that it appears there is little reason to be a Christian at all. What is distinct about a Christianity that is indistinguishable from the world's vision of the good life?

Our customizable versions of following Jesus today reflect our own wants, desires, and beliefs. Christian teachings and doctrine are now malleable to the culture, hoping to gain acceptance, not realizing that acceptance from the culture should never have been our goal to begin with. This is the state of Christianity for most Americans.

RAPID CHANGE

Things change fast. Most Americans in the early 2000s viewed homosexuality and same-sex marriage as unnatural and immoral. The church and the culture matched each other in these beliefs. Most politicians, including Democrats, recognized marriage as belonging only to one man and one woman. Barack Obama, Bill and Hillary Clinton, and other prominent liberal politicians supported traditional marriage. But then the cultural winds changed direction.

Activism by the gay and lesbian community, combined with persuasion from music, movies, and television shows, turned public opinion. I'll never forget the movie *I Now Pronounce You Chuck and Larry*. Adam

Sandler and Kevin James play two straight men who pretend to be gay in order to ensure James' character can provide insurance for his children. The moral of the 2007 film is that these two guys realize how much homophobic animosity exists in the world, especially from Christians. I remember being stunned by how effectively the storyline was crafted to "normalize" homosexuality, all while framing Christians as the enemy to that normalization.

Efforts to normalize homosexuality gained momentum in the United States, just as they had done throughout Europe years earlier. Politicians soon jumped on the bandwagon. Then, in 2015, the Supreme Court ruled in the landmark *Obergefell v. Hodges* case that same-sex couples had a fundamental right to marry under the Fourteenth Amendment of the Constitution. And with that ruling, the sexual revolution steamed ahead. Transgender rights became the next discussion, as well as polyamory, polygamy, and other perversions of God's wise, good, and beautiful design for gender and sexuality.

The culture's message and tone around these topics has shifted dramatically since this time. It progressed from a plea for rights and toleration to outright demands for affirmation and celebration. You can no longer disagree, even respectfully, without being subjected to name-calling, the maligning of your character, even being "canceled."

WHO'S INFLUENCING WHOM

What were Christians doing while all these changes occurred? Some stood firm and proclaimed a biblical ethic of sexuality and still do to this day. But many shifted in their beliefs. In the face of tremendous cultural pressure, many professing Christians "re-evaluated" their convictions on the subject. And the result? Lots of Christians abandoned the idea that God created sex to be experienced and expressed in an exclusive relationship between one man and one woman in a marriage covenant. Some went further. They denied the Bible taught such an ethic at all.

Arguments emerged to fit the prevailing winds of culture. People claimed Paul's multiple condemnations of homosexuality (Romans 1:26-27, 1 Corinthians 6:9) had been misunderstood. Some argued Paul only meant to condemn pederasty (sexual activity involving a man and a young boy), a practice common in Greek and Roman culture. He was not, or so this reasoning goes, condemning homosexual couples in "monogamous and consensual" relationships—only abusive ones. This view claims Paul lacked any concept of same-sex marriage as it exists in America, where individuals commit to one another as faithful partners. Therefore, according to this deeply flawed logic, Paul is not condemning what is happening in today's culture in the biblical passages that indicate those who practice homosexuality will not inherit the kingdom of God.

Other people argue homosexuality is compatible

with Christianity because Jesus never condemned homosexuality. This is an argument from silence: "Since Jesus doesn't explicitly condemn homosexuality, Christians can't say God disapproves of it". But this ignores Jesus' teaching on marriage in Matthew 19 where He links marriage back to creation in Genesis 2. Jesus affirms God created our first parents as male and female, and recounts Moses' words that a man shall leave his father and mother and hold fast to his wife. The only language Jesus ever uses to describe marriage is a man and a woman.

Those who push to harmonize Christianity and homosexuality argue that Jesus was only affirming the first-century norm in His culture. They claim Jesus isn't really "reaffirming" the idea of marriage as one man and one woman. Instead, He was just speaking about marriage as He and His culture understood it at the time. But this implies Jesus was like any other man —nothing more than a product of His time and place in history—and not God in the flesh. The argument fails. If Jesus is God, declaring the end from the beginning (Isaiah 46:10), then He was aware our present hour in Western history would come. He knew we would debate this subject. Jesus didn't need to condemn same-sex marriage because He reaffirmed the only true definition of marriage. Jesus' reaffirmation of biblical marriage is the very reason Christians are not free to redefine marriage or celebrate homosexuality.

However, despite the weakness of these arguments, many American Christians have caved to the cultural pressure to approve of homosexuality. The constant preaching and discipling of the culture has influenced Christians more than the preaching and discipling of the church. Instead of Christians influencing the world on this subject, the world has been influencing us.

SOLID CHURCH KID

Not long ago, one pastor at my church had breakfast with a college student who was previously in our youth ministry. The kid has great parents, knows his Bible, and possesses a solid spiritual foundation, more solid than most people his age.

During the meal with our pastor, the young man shared his struggles with the Bible's teachings on homosexuality. He wasn't gay, nor did he have any struggles with same-sex attraction, but he found a group of friends that saw no problem with being gay and being Christian at the same time. His gay friends didn't view homosexuality as something against God's commands. They thought the church should accept them just as they are.

The student read and studied the arguments in favor of God accepting homosexuality but didn't find them persuasive. Yet, he still struggled to affirm what the Bible taught. Even when he knew the Bible taught against it, having friends who were pro-homosexuality held tremendous sway over his convictions. How is this possible with someone we considered solid and ready to face the onslaught of cultural pressures?

I shared this story at a parenting conference in Florida and had a man approach me afterwards. He and his wife were in the same position. Their son grew up in the church, knew the Bible, and helped lead in student ministry. He had since gone to college at the University of Florida, got around a group of friends who affirmed homosexuality, with some identifying as gay, and he changed his beliefs. The son is not even sure if he's a Christian anymore. And the father wept as he told me the story.

Personal relationships with people shape our perspectives on things. That's not a surprise. However, if we were great friends with someone who committed murder or robbed a store, we wouldn't question whether murder or stealing was bad. We know those things are objectively wrong. So why should having a friend who is gay change our convictions about what God says on the subject? It shouldn't. Being friends with a drug addict shouldn't change our view about drugs, no matter how much joy our friend tells us the drugs give him. We know drugs destroy a person. But we struggle to remember that going against God's design for sexuality and marriage also destroys people. I have no doubt this is why the rates of anxiety, depression, and suicide are astronomical in the LGBTQ+ community. There is no peace for living in open defiance of God's design and commands.

Why was this young man our pastor met with struggling so much over this issue? Why do so many professing Christians now affirm homosexuality when they considered it a grievous sin only ten years ago? The Bible hasn't changed. The beliefs of the church over the last 2,000 years haven't changed. So, what changed? The culture.

When most Americans disapproved of homosexuality and gay marriage, most Christians did too. But now that most Americans approve of homosexuality and gay marriage, many Christians are changing their views. Professing Christians are struggling over what they believe. Why the struggle? Why now? Because to go against the culture's doctrine on sexuality costs you something. The pressure to conform has grown stronger. The weight of standing against the culture is a load too heavy to bear for many Christians. The result? Conformity to the culture.

Why is that? Why do the statistics say more will do so as time goes on? That's the subject of our next chapter.

Discussion Questions

1. Does the teaching you most often hear focus on life advice or the Gospel of Christ? What does the real Gospel give that a false gospel can't?

2. How would you define "happiness"? How does your view of happiness measure up to scriptural definitions?

3. How do the movies, books, and TV shows you watch impact the way you feel about gender and sexuality? List them below.

4. Christians are sometimes accused of focusing on homosexuality or transgenderism over other sins. Why are those specific sins such a focus for the church today?

5. Do you find your views on sex and gender are impacted more by the people around you or God's word?

4

THE EASY BUTTON

Today there are so many ideas and philosophies being propagated by pop-culture, the media, and schools that we Christians absorb and adopt without thought. Too often, Christians are quick to affirm ideas preached by the culture without ever discerning the roots of those ideas. We are unequipped to recognize concepts and philosophies that stem from godless ideologies.

Words like cisgender, intersectionality, heteronormativity, white fragility, white privilege, and others have entered the lexicon of our culture in recent years, seemingly out of nowhere. But there is a worldview undergirding these terms. They are downstream from a source. The short-hand description of this way of seeing the world is "woke."

When I attended Vanderbilt Divinity School in 2007, this ideology drove all the lectures and assigned reading. I didn't know the origins of these ideas; they were just the accepted way of thinking and talking about things. It was the air you breathed inside the halls and classrooms of that institution. And it didn't take long for me to realize how out of step those things were with my own convictions.

I soon left Vanderbilt to pursue seminary education elsewhere. But not long after that, I knew something strange was happening when I began hearing similar ideas and language coming from the mouths of the evangelical leaders I fled to when I left Vanderbilt. People I counted as trusted voices began to sound like my former professors and classmates.

The philosophy underneath many of these ideas being popularized today is Critical Theory. These concepts lived secluded in institutions of higher learning for decades, rarely spilling outside of those circles. But around 2015, following the shooting death of Michael Brown, these ideas exploded into the mainstream.

What had lived undetected within universities for years finally came out into the open. Every corner of society started speaking the same message. Countless politicians, athletes, musicians, actors, and activists were suddenly playing from the same sheet of music. And as they began singing the same notes, the media turned the volume up so loud everyone had to listen. The ideas originating from Critical Theory sprang into America's consciousness.

CRITICAL THEORY

Critical Theory has its origins in Frankfurt, Germany at Goethe University, which was founded in 1923 with the purpose of developing Marxist studies. When the Nazis came into power, they forced the school to close in 1933 and it moved to Columbia University in New York City. Notice again that its purpose was to further Marxist studies. The Marx in "Marxist studies" is Karl Marx, the German philosopher who birthed the philosophical foundations of communism. Critical Theory, an approach to social analysis, functions as a comprehensive worldview. Today, there are many branches of study underneath the general heading of Critical Theory: Critical Race Theory (CRT), Feminism, LGBTQ issues, Postcolonial Theory, Postmodernism, and cultural studies.

Many dispute the dangers of Critical Theory, particularly Critical Race Theory, because they claim it is only a legal theory. It isn't incorrect to say CRT has its roots in legal theory. CRT developed in the 1970s and 1980s because legal scholars, lawyers, and activists believed the advances of the Civil Rights Movement of the 1960s had ceased. The focus became challenging the conventional legal strategies as incapable of providing social and economic justice for minorities. A basic tenet of CRT is that racism is embedded into society and affects, not just an individual disposition or a degenerate few, but everything. CRT advocates do not believe the law could correct the problem, because the law is a part of a system that was designed to perpetuate the oppression of minorities.

People who insist CRT is "just a legal theory" are either being naïve or misleading. Yes, it started as a legal theory, but its basic assumptions have spread far beyond the realm of law. It is no longer just a legal discussion; it morphed into a more comprehensive view of the world. And the premises established by CRT have now lodged into the minds and consciences of many.

Here's why this matters: Once the premises are accepted, they quickly spill out of the arena of law and touch everything else. Racism permeates not just the legal system but every system. Minorities are denied legal justice because they were denied power. Everything is now a struggle for power. It becomes the measure of justice and equality. The idea was too insidious to remain in its cage. And it didn't. Once we let it out, it ate everything.

The moment you adopt the approach of seeing everything through the lens of power: every individual becomes either the oppressed or oppressor. And this is not based on any person's actual actions, opinions, beliefs, or behavior—only on their race. But Critical Theory itself goes even further to label everyone according to their race, class, gender, sexuality, and even religion. Oppression happens when dominant groups impose their norms and values on others. This is what intersectionality (an outworking of Critical Theory) teaches us to believe. A woman ranks higher than a man on the intersectionality matrix; however, a white heterosexual Christian woman is quickly surpassed by a man who is black, homosexual, and non-Christian. Why? Because he has more oppressed and minority badges to claim than she does. She's now an oppressor. That's how this game is played.

BIG PROBLEMS

I hope you see why this ideology is so dangerous. It runs counter to the teachings of Scripture. In fact, according to this ideology, Christianity is an "oppressor" religion. Islam is a minority religion, so it ranks higher in the intersectionality chart.

In this scheme, truth is not objective, and ideas are not tested on their own merits. Rather, it depends on who is making a claim that determines its veracity. Critical Theory rejects claims about "absolute truth" as veiled attempts to preserve the oppressor's power and privilege. This tactic conveniently allows for critics of Critical Theory to be ignored. After all, privileged groups are blinded by their privilege, making their claims invalid. This is a clever way of silencing anyone who doesn't rank high enough on the intersectionality chart. Oppressed groups have access to truth through their lived experience as oppressed people. That experience and perspective trumps all other evidence of truth.

The danger in this discussion is that many of the

same words and concepts Christians affirm (justice, antiracism, equality) are also used by those promoting Critical Theory. If we're not careful, we can think we're talking about the same things, rooted in the same foundations. But we're not. And it is easy to understand how so many well-intentioned Christians have been sucked in by this ideology.

This thinking isn't going away. It's not new; it's been around for a while. But it's becoming increasingly popular. And it has now spilled into pop-culture, the education system, and the media. Even professing Christians are buying into it. In fact, it's becoming more difficult for Christians to speak against these ideas and concepts without being labeled "fundamentalists." This quip dismisses critiques offered against these concepts as fear-mongering over a non-existent boogeyman.

But this boogeyman is real.

They catechize these ideas into the culture through music, movies, shows, social media, education, and sports. Besides being called a fundamentalist, speaking against it or denying its truth can also earn you labels like racist, misogynist, transphobic, or homophobic.

Recently, "Chrissy" Stroop, a trans woman (biological male), reprimanded Baylor Professor Beth Allison Barr on Twitter. Barr was trying to be an "ally" amid a dust up with Stroop's endorsement of a controversial book, which claimed white evangelicals have corrupted Christianity. But because Barr suggested people should be nice to others even if they disagreed with their "life choice," Stroop shot back a turgid response that those who disagreed are bigots.[2] Even respectful disagreement will not shield you from name-calling and reprimands. Being an ally requires full-throated affirmation or you're an enemy—just a bigot.

Still, not a few professing evangelicals have tried at all costs to win acceptance and approval from such extreme progressive voices. I call these evangelicals progressive-lite. These folks claim to hold a biblical sexual ethic, but never talk about it and refuse to criticize the damage of the LGBTQ+ revolution (e.g., Beth Allison Barr apologized to "Chrissy" Stroop and then deleted her tweets).

These professing believers seldom criticize unbiblical expressions of gender or marriage, but freely criticize the slightest perversion of the complementarian view. Many of these folks profess to be politically neutral, but rarely criticize harmful liberal policies and positions, while regularly distancing themselves from conservative political views. Some have propagated media falsehoods about conservatives, even disseminating misinformation in the name of "loving their

---

2 Stroop, Chrissy [@c_stroop]. (2022, February 24). I mean, people who disagree with my "life choice" to transition are bigots. Full stop. For many, many trans people, the other option is suicide. Queerness isn't a choice [Tweet]. Twitter. twitter.com/c_stroop/status/1496884781912510465?s=21

neighbor."[3]

These progressive-lite evangelicals have swallowed much of the framework and lenses of Critical Theory. They still confess orthodox doctrinal beliefs yet seem to use a different matrix for how they live. They confess one thing and live another.

Remember Paul's words to the church in Colossae:

See to it that no one takes you captive by philosophy and empty deceit, according to human tradition, according to the elemental spirits of the world, and not according to Christ. — Colossians 2:8

We must pay attention and see to it that no one takes us captive through vain philosophies and empty deceits. Why does this require careful attention? Because we are all prone to it. But we can't let these ideas take us captive.

In combat, armies lead away captives of war as spoil. That's what happens when we conform to the culture. We are led away as spoil won by the world. The philosophies of the world are being preached all around us. They are everywhere. How do we know when we are dealing with such ideas? We must train ourselves to recognize ideas and ideologies that are

---

[3] https://www.dailywire.com/news/how-the-federal-government-used-evangelical-leaders-to-spread-covid-propaganda-to-churches

according to the world and not of Christ. We must test whether such things align with Scripture. If I can sum up Paul's point, he says: don't get sucked into ways of thinking and living that originate from fallen men and demons instead of grounding yourself in the Word and ways of Christ.

Be on guard. Fight the drift.

FALSE CONVERTS

How is it that so many professing Christians can conform their beliefs to match the prevailing views of the culture?

One answer some give is that such people are not really believers. That is possible. False converts are a real phenomenon. There are people who profess to be Christians, perhaps even demonstrating evidence they are, but then they fall away.

As a pastor for many years now, I've watched this happen. People blow in and get excited about the things of God for a season, maybe even cleaning some sin issues up in their lives, and then blow out as quickly as they arrived. Jesus tells a parable about seeds sown into the ground that shoot up, but then wither because there is no depth of soil (Matthew 13:3-9). John writes that some in the church went out from among the body because they were never a part of the body (1 John 2:19). Both Jesus and John show that there are always weeds among the wheat of the church (Matthew 13:24-30). Not everyone who professes

Christ loves Christ. Not all who claim to follow Jesus actually do.

But that reason alone is not enough to understand why so many Christians conform to the culture. Calling every person an unbeliever who struggles with holding biblical beliefs in the face of a culture going in the opposite direction is too simple. Yes, some conform because they are not real Christians. But there is more going on here.

Do you want to know why, statistically speaking, most professing Christians in high school today will walk away from the faith within two years of graduating? Do you want to know why more and more adult believers will find their beliefs aligning with the culture?

Because it's easy.

That's the answer. Most conform, and many struggle with wanting to conform because it's just easier. It's easier to conform and find acceptance from the culture than it is to go against the grain. Swimming upstream is hard work. Forfeiting acceptance from the world or your friends is far more difficult than most of us want to admit.

LOSING ACCEPTANCE

Losing acceptance is unacceptable for most people. If we're honest, the cost of losing acceptance is just too high a price for most of us to pay. We like being liked. And I'm the same way. There are few people who enjoy being disliked or an outcast. Normal people enjoy acceptance.

Our nature and instincts are to blend in. Few of us enjoy standing out from the crowd. This is why everyone gets embarrassed by their former hairstyle or outfit when looking at old photos. That version of you wouldn't fit in today. But notice that in those old photos, everyone looks the same. And the collective style is a direct reflection on the cultural fashions of that time.

Fashions and fads in clothing, home interiors, graphics, and other things come and go. Most people, ourselves included, just follow the trends. We have iPhones. Only a few use other brands. Three of you are still using a flip-phone. Yet at one time, the flip-phone was the iPhone. Why do most people own iPhones? Not because the iPhone is the best technology on the market, but because that's what everyone uses. It is the popular choice.

Why do we watch the movies and shows others are talking about? Why do we listen to the same music as others? Why do we buy the brands we do? There may be legitimate reasons for each of these things but mixed in the equation is our longing for acceptance. We want to fit in.

That isn't necessarily sinful. But it does make staying faithful to the Bible difficult. Conformity is easier than resisting. Embracing the same name brands and copying trends in the culture is common for all, but the challenge comes when we need the courage to separate ourselves.

Christians must listen to what God says about what is true, beautiful, and good. The struggle arises when what God says about truth, beauty, and goodness conflicts with what the world believes. Are we willing to affirm God's Word, or do we conform to the culture?

APPROVAL JUNKIES

The same Apostle Paul who wrote to the church in Rome not to conform to the world (Romans 12:2) gave a similar warning to the church in Galatia. Paul writes this to the believers there:

For am I now seeking the approval of man, or of God? Or am I trying to please man? If I were still trying to please man, I would not be a servant of Christ. — Galatians 1:10

This verse begins with a rhetorical question. Is Paul seeking the approval of man or of God? Well, he is an apostle of Jesus, so the answer is clear. He lives for God's approval over man's approval. He then asks if he's trying to please man. But why is he even asking these questions?

After Paul planted a church among the Galatians, people followed behind him, teaching doctrines and ideas contrary to the gospel Paul taught them. The church in Galatia found itself tossed back and forth over what to believe. They turned to a different gospel from the time Paul preached to them to the time of his writing his letter. They strayed away from sound teaching.

When Paul writes them, he is not looking to win a popularity contest. He doesn't compete with the false teachers who followed behind him to be the most liked. His goal isn't to change his doctrines in order to gain the approval of the church in Galatia. No, he seeks God's approval above theirs, and it's only because he wants to please God that he can serve the Galatian believers at all.

He tells them why his stance is so firm: if he were still trying to please man, he wouldn't be a servant of Christ. There was a time when Paul lived to please man. Before his conversion, his zeal raged to assist the other Jewish leaders in their efforts to squash the gospel. Paul wanted to play his part in stomping out the people who claimed Jesus as Lord. But then he came to faith in Jesus. When Paul converted to Christianity, there was no living to serve anyone but Christ. Serving and pleasing man no longer received any of Paul's attention. Jesus had his focus, loyalty, and devotion.

Paul recognized that living to please man disqualified him from serving Christ. Disciples of Jesus serve the Master. Jesus is King, no other. Those who follow Christ cannot pledge their allegiance to serving the world or man above Christ. Paul saw conformity as disqualifying from serving Jesus. If Paul were living to please man, he would not be a servant of Christ.

Notice how strong the language is here. He doesn't say it would be hard or difficult to be a servant of Christ if he were living to please man. He says he couldn't be: "I would not be a servant of Christ." There is no confusion in his message. The clarity of this passage should prompt reflection and consideration in us. This truth is not true just for Paul; it's true for us. If we live our lives to please man, we cannot be servants of Christ. If we pursue the approval of men over God, we will not be servants of Christ.

This should convict us. Most of us are approval junkies who need to let these words call us to confession and repentance. We want to be liked way too much. Many of us profess to serve Christ, but our words, beliefs, and actions show we live to please man.

The temptation facing Christians is to conform to the ways of the world. The cultural pressure to conform aligns with our heart's natural desire to fit in and find acceptance. Most people will conform, and many Christians have conformed already. Why? It's just easier.

That prospect looms over each of us. We must resolve to serve Christ above living to please others. We must desire God's approval more than the approval of man. Resolving that in our hearts today is the focus of the next chapter.

Discussion Questions

1. What is Critical Theory?

2. In what areas of have you personally seen Critical Theory applied (e.g., at work, at school, in the media)?

3. Read Galatians 3:27-29. How does the "ranking" by race, sexuality, and other factors contrast with what the Bible says about who we are in Christ?

4. How do definitions of justice, anti-racism, and equality differ for proponents of Critical Theory vs. those who hold to biblical principles?

5. From whom are you most tempted to seek acceptance and approval? What biblical truths can you preach to yourself to help you turn from this?

5

CONTEND FOR THE FAITH

Winston Churchill is the reason you are not speaking German in a Nazi-ruled world today. His willingness to confront Adolf Hitler without blinking made him different. He rallied England to resist the temptation to surrender their island to Germany without a fight. His courage and leadership during World War II stands as one of the greatest examples and inspiring stories in human history.

Churchill did not become the Prime Minister of the United Kingdom until May 10th, 1940. By that time, the Nazi war machine had swept through most of Europe and taken possession of Czechoslovakia, Poland, Denmark, Norway, Belgium, the Netherlands, Luxembourg, and was on the verge of taking France. Most of Europe had underestimated the might of the German military, as well as the insatiable thirst for power of Adolf Hitler. Churchill's predecessor, Neville Chamberlain, had failed to grasp Hitler's ambitions and, as a result, the German army's advance now posed a significant threat to England.

Having failed to stop or placate Hitler, Chamberlain resigned his office. Churchill was called upon to lead. He got to work immediately, but Churchill soon discovered that senior officials in the government expected him to negotiate peace terms with Hitler to avoid bombing and fighting on English soil. But Churchill refused. He would not capitulate or surrender. He resolved to lead. He was determined that England would fight against Hitler, even if they had to fight alone.

Churchill inspired the citizens of the British Empire to stand up and fight. His speeches to Parliament and the nation via radio, and his commitment to take the fight to Hitler, provided the strength for resistance that the British people needed. One of those speeches is still remembered as a masterpiece of oratory. It is called "We Shall Fight on the Beaches."

Churchill made the speech on June 4, 1940, only a few weeks after becoming Prime Minister.[4] France had fallen. The German army occupied Paris. Everyone knew Hitler's sights would now turn to the island nation across the English Channel. Potential invasion by air, sea, or both was looming in the minds of British citizens. And the devastating nighttime bombings from

---

[4] Read the entire speech at: https://winstonchurchill.org/resources/speeches/1940-the-finest-hour/we-shall-fight-on-the-beaches/

the German Luftwaffe (Air Force) would soon commence. Facing this reality, Churchill delivered this historic twenty-minute speech, with an ending that enraptured the hearts and minds of his fearful listeners.

At his conclusion, Churchill said, "We shall go on to the end, we shall fight in France, we shall fight on the seas and oceans, we shall fight with growing confidence and growing strength in the air, we shall defend our Island, whatever the cost may be, we shall fight on the beaches, we shall fight on the landing grounds, we shall fight in the fields and in the streets, we shall fight in the hills; we shall never surrender, and even if, which I do not for a moment believe, this Island or a large part of it were subjugated and starving, then our Empire beyond the seas, armed and guarded by the British Fleet, would carry on the struggle, until, in God's good time, the New World, with all its power and might, steps forth to the rescue and the liberation of the old."

These words, delivered to the House of Commons and broadcast by radio to the nation, steeled the resolve of the British people. There was no longer any doubt whether Britain would continue the fight. Talk of appeasement dissipated. The courageous words and defiant leadership of Britain's new Prime Minister marked the turning point of the war. Churchill's willingness to confront the enemy, rather than appease him, spearheaded the defeat of the Nazis in 1945—a defeat that liberated Europe and ultimately saved countless millions from tyranny.

ADVERSARIES & FOES

Winston Churchill led England through the darkest days imaginable. The enemy surrounded and threatened them on all sides. He delivered tough words to inspire the people. But more than that, he took action. Every other nation was crushed under Germany's might. Yet Churchill led England to strive for the survival of their island and the preservation of their freedom.

He ramped up production of British aircraft to protect the island from the relentless bombings of the German Luftwaffe. England labored to crack the code of German navigational systems. And Churchill ordered all air defense missiles sent to the city for more protection and defense. When the Germans bombed London, Churchill responded by dropping bombs on Berlin, something the rest of the world—including the German people—believed to be impossible. Churchill refused to cower or remain idle as the German war machine turned its sights upon his people. With courage and conviction he stood against Hitler. It turned the tide of the war.

It takes people of courage and conviction to stand up to adversaries. Adversaries will always exist. In this world, there are not only geo-political enemies, but spiritual ones. The apostle Paul understood this. He reminded the church of Ephesus to stand strong against the schemes of the devil (Ephesians 6:11). Satan, the adversary, prowls around seeking people to devour (1 Peter 5:8). The Christian life is a struggle filled with battles and skirmishes against spiritual foes. These are not imagined or metaphorical battles and foes. They are real.

Paul writes in Ephesians 6:12, "For our struggle is not against flesh and blood, but against the rulers, against the authorities, against the powers of this world's darkness, and against the spiritual forces of evil in the heavenly realms." In terms of spiritual warfare, Paul isn't describing this conflict as some type of horror movie like *The Exorcist* (though evil spirits can possess people and manifest in dark ways). These spiritual adversaries and foes cause destruction through everyday means, including other people. Hitler is a great example of this. His entire ideology was wicked. Yet we don't need the example of Hitler to recognize how Satan uses unbiblical ideas to bring destruction in the world.

An example of this plays out in Acts 20. Here we learn Paul is about to travel to Jerusalem, where he knows the religious leaders wait to arrest him. He stops at the island of Miletus and calls for the elders in the church of Ephesus to visit him. There, he gives them a charge. He knows it is his last time with them, which weights his words with significance. In Acts 20:29, Paul tells these leaders, "I know that after my departure fierce wolves will come in among you, not sparing the flock; and from among your own selves will arise men speaking twisted things, to draw away the disciples after them."

Paul warns the church of Ephesus that fierce wolves are coming after his departure. These wolves are not coming with violence or physical aggression against the church. No, they are going to present twisted ideas as truth. And as a result, these wolves will draw disciples away from the church. That's what wolves do. They are adversaries and foes who devour the sheep.

Paul says these wolves will not spare the flock. But is he saying the church should run and hide? No. Is he telling the church to disband and avoid being devoured? No. Is it possible he means the church should celebrate what the wolves are teaching and join them? Of course not. He tells them to be alert (vs 31) and to pay careful attention to themselves and the flock (vs 28). He is warning them so they will be prepared to contend for the faith against the wolves.

These adversaries and foes of biblical truth are not only present outside of the church. We know there is hostility against our beliefs, especially when they conflict with the culture's beliefs about sexuality, gender, abortion, and any number of issues. But we are wrong to assume adversaries and foes are only outsiders. One of the greatest threats the church faces today is from adversaries "on the inside." John Piper once said, "The wolves who pervert the faith are professing Christians.

They are pastors and church leaders and seminary teachers and missionaries."[5] These insider wolves are those who, by their speaking and writing and example, lead Christians astray from the faith.

JOIN THE STRUGGLE

In Jude 3 we read the thesis of the entire letter:

"Beloved, although I was very eager to write to you about our common salvation, I found it necessary to write appealing to you to contend for the faith that was once for all delivered to the saints."

Jude was the half-brother of Jesus. He writes to Christians about defending the faith and standing firm against false teachers and false teaching. The verse we just read is the thesis of the entire letter.

Jude exhorts these Christians to contend for the faith. The word "contend," in the original Greek that Jude wrote it in, points to action involved in a competition or contest. It's focused action, skilled activity. The word signals a struggle to oppose something. The literal translation of contend is to "struggle upon appropriately." Therefore, the word is supposed to make us think of competitions or contests, where two sides are vying for supremacy and victory. Churchill con-

---

[5] https://www.desiringgod.org/messages/contend-for-the-faith

tended for Britain's survival. He was engaged in a fierce struggle of skill and commitment against Nazi Germany.

Why does Jude choose "contend" as the verb to describe their actions? Because, like Paul's warning to the Ephesus elders, Jude knows there are false teachers who want to lead people astray. There are wolves setting themselves up as teachers of the sheep. That is why Jude tells them to contend "for the faith that was once for all delivered to the saints."

It is the faith we are to contend for. There is a body of doctrine and beliefs that make up the Christian faith. We often call this "the truth" or "the gospel," but it is shorthand for the Christian message. Notice that Jude says it is a faith "once for all delivered to the saints." This phrase shows its unchanging nature. It's impossible for this message to shift or morph with time. That is why the church must contend for it.

John Gill says Jude's words in verse 3 denote "a conflict, a combat, or a fighting for it, striving even to an agony."[6] Contend here is a graphic word that should catch our attention with the force Jude intended it to supply. For the church to contend for the faith in our day means the same thing it did when Jude first wrote these words: fight for its defense.

The faith is worth fighting for. The faith we pro-

---

[6] https://www.biblestudytools.com/commentaries/gills-exposition-of-the-bible/jude-1-3.html

claim is the power of God to save sinners (Romans 1:16). It is a body of doctrine and truth delivered by the mouth of God Himself, which alone can equip us for every good work (2 Timothy 3:16-17). This faith sustains weak and weary sinners and reminds us of all the promises of God in Christ.

Adversaries will arise. They have risen since the beginning. These wolves deny the faith once for all delivered to the saints. They embrace sin and teach against the clear directives of Scripture. They pervert and twist biblical truth with false doctrines and counterfeit gospels. Some of this is seen in today's "deconstruction" movement, where many Christians are questioning or critically examining their beliefs, with some making significant changes and others walking away from the faith entirely.

Pastor Josh Howerton distinguishes between two kinds of deconstruction. The deconstruction that is healthy versus the unhealthy.[7] The healthy is a detachment from dead religion and the embracing of the actual teachings of Scripture: "you have heard it said, but

---

[7] Howerton, Josh [@howertonjosh]. (2022, February 17). There are legitimately 2 types of people self-identifying under the deconstruction label CATEGORY 1: people doing healthy "you have heard it said, but I say unto you" detachment FROM dead religion and cults and TO the teachings of the Scriptures. CATEGORY 2: people with thinly-veiled defiance and hostility to the clear teachings of the Scriptures. They are often using secular categories to evaluate the violently non-secular Scriptures and deconstructing not just systems, but faith and Biblical ethics themselves. [Tweet]. Twitter. twitter.com/howertonjosh/status/1494439454735577091?s=11

I say unto you..." The unhealthy is a "thinly veiled defiance and hostility to the clear teaching of the Scriptures which uses secular categories to evaluate the Scriptures, deconstructing not just systems, but faith and Biblical ethics themselves." Josh is right. That second deconstruction kills biblical faith, and the people promoting it are dangerous — wolves.

AN ALL SKATE

When I was a kid, skating rinks were big. We took school trips to the skating rink. The daycare took us to the skating rink. People had their birthday parties at the skating rink. Eighties kids either learned to skate or spent their time watching everyone else skate to Vanilla Ice and MC Hammer.

A large portion of time each day at the skating rink included games and competitions. The games singled out different age groups and genders for races, limbo, tag, and other contests. But after these finished, the DJ would announce over the PA system that it was an all skate. This meant everyone could skate again, so we all made our way back to the wooden surface and took laps as the music blared.

Contending for the faith is an "all skate" activity. It doesn't single out highly gifted church members. No, Jude's exhortation is for all true believers. The question is not whether we should all contend for the faith, but how we should contend for the faith. In light of this, I'm going to offer three ways we can start contending for the faith in our lives.

First, know the faith. We cannot contend for the faith that was once for all delivered to the saints if we do not know what the faith is. There is a knowledge base that this faith contains, found in the Scriptures, that we must know and understand if we want to contend faithfully. This means we need to study the Scriptures. We need to read for ourselves and listen to others explain the Scriptures to develop a comprehensive theology of what the Bible teaches. We need to commit ourselves to continuous growth in our grasp of the Bible's teachings. This will teach us to discern the truthfulness of the arguments and ideas we encounter through that lens.

Second, pray. Throughout Jesus' earthly ministry, He stopped to pray (Luke 9:18). His work of teaching, healing, and battling against the kingdom of darkness was a picture of contending. But He didn't do it without prayer. We need to make time daily to pray as we contend for the faith. Pray for your family and your church to stay the course. Pray for opportunities to engage in conversations about the gospel. Ask God for conviction and courage to speak up when you hear or see wolves twisting and distorting the truth.

Third, share your faith. We contend as we speak the truth of the gospel to those who do not follow Christ. Later in his letter, Jude tells his readers (vs 23) to "save others by snatching them out of the fire; to others show mercy with fear, hating even the garment stained by the flesh." We contend for the faith when we seek to rescue people from the clutches of the enemy and show them the forgiveness and redemption found in Christ alone.

RESOLVE IT NOW

The secret of Winston Churchill's success in standing toe-to-toe against Hitler and the German military was his resolve to fight before the fight showed up. He determined England would not settle for appeasement, regardless of what terms Hitler offered. Churchill didn't trust Hitler to keep any promises. He knew his word was as worthless as the paper they would draft the peace treaty on. No, as long as Churchill was Prime Minister, he would not capitulate. He stood firm. He decided in advance that Britain would fight, even if they fought alone.

The church today needs the same resolve. We must decide in advance to contend for the faith once for all delivered to the saints. We can only resist the bombardment of cultural pressures and internal draw to conformity when we decide in advance we are not moving off the line. Our mindsets matter. We must know where we stand. We must know what we believe. Even if we must stand alone, resolve to stand regardless.

Moses' farewell speech to the people of Israel in Deuteronomy 30 has this flare. He knows his life is nearing its end. The people have a choice before them.

They can choose life and obey God, following His statutes as He has outlined, or they can choose death by rejecting Him. The choice is theirs, but he implores them with a soul-stirring exhortation to choose life.

In Deuteronomy 30:19-20 Moses says, "I call heaven and earth to witness against you today, that I have set before you life and death, blessing and curse. Therefore choose life, that you and your offspring may live, loving the Lord your God, obeying his voice and holding fast to him, for he is your life and length of days, that you may dwell in the land that the Lord swore to your fathers, to Abraham, to Isaac, and to Jacob, to give them." Therefore, choose life! Make the choice now! Don't wait until you are facing a trial or temptation. Decide now to choose life and then live under that choice.

This is the call for us as believers. We must make the choice to contend for the faith rather than conforming to the culture. The pull toward conformity will confront every one of us. We must choose now that we won't back down. We must settle our hearts now that we will join the struggle. May God give us the courage to do so, because we have something worth defending far greater than an island.

Discussion Questions

1. What does it mean to "contend for the faith"?

2. In what ways do you see yourself called to "contend for the faith"?

3. Why must Christians be ready to contend both within and outside of the church?

4. Do you feel confident in being able to share and defend the gospel? If not, who are people in your life with whom you might learn to contend for the faith?

5. How should we respond to the current movement toward "faith deconstruction" in light of Jude's admonition to "contend for the faith"?

6

BE TRANSFORMED

I became a Christian when I was nine years old. My parents didn't attend church, but I stayed with my grandmother on Saturdays and went to church with her. I attended Sunday school class for an hour and then went to "big church" with my grandmother. Each Sunday I sat on the pew with my grandmother, alternating between doodling on the bulletin program and laying in her lap.

After the sermon, the pastor stood at the front waiting for people who needed to "make a decision for Christ" to come down. One Sunday, after he finished, I felt the urge to go down front. Some of my friends had already "prayed to receive Jesus." I didn't know much about the Bible, but I believed the basics of Christianity to be true. I also believed my need for forgiveness through Jesus was real.

"Just As I Am" played as it did each week. I stepped into the aisle, walked down to the pastor, and said, "I want to follow Jesus and be a Christian." The pastor prayed with me and announced it to the church. Everyone clapped and celebrated my decision and congratulated me. After the service concluded, the pastor took me to his office and asked me a bunch of questions about sin, my beliefs about Jesus, and other basic questions to ensure I understood what I had done. I did. A few weeks later, the church baptized me in the name of the Father, Son, and Holy Spirit.

CONFORMED

After my profession of faith and baptism, I continued life as normal for a young boy. I played sports, attended church with my grandmother on Sundays, and went to school. No big changes.

However, while nothing changed about my daily life, two significant things took place over time. First, I didn't grow in my knowledge and understanding of being a Christian. I kept going to Sunday school and hearing the same Bible stories I heard every year. "Big church" sermons made little sense to me. As I entered my teenage years, my understanding of being a Christian was about the same as when I walked the aisle as a nine-year-old.

The second significant development during this time was my growing desire to fit in with a particular friend group. I wanted to be liked and accepted. As we got older, the temptations to sin and rebel grew larger. I first viewed pornography at twelve years old. We started chewing smokeless tobacco. Impressing girls dominated our minds. My relationship with my parents tanked as I fought for more freedom and autonomy from their rules. As a fourteen-year-old freshman in high school, I started drinking and smoking marijuana. Within a few years, my life looked very different from what it did before. I never attended church through middle school or high school.

What happened to me? Why did I run in this direction? I conformed to the patterns of my friends because I wanted their acceptance above everything. This continued throughout my entire time in high school, until twenty years old, when the Lord (through a series of circumstances) brought me to the end of my rebellion. When Jesus brought me to repentance, my life changed, and my desires shifted to pleasing God more than anyone else.

But when I look back at my life, from coming to faith at nine years old to running into full-blown rebellion by twelve years old, it's easy to trace what went wrong. Nobody discipled me. Nobody ever showed me how to follow Jesus. And nobody prepared me for the onslaught of worldly temptation awaiting me a few short years after my salvation.

Couple my anemic understanding of following Jesus with a growing desire to fit in with my friends, and you get the rebellion and sin I embraced in those years. I conformed. As I reflect on those developments in my life, it doesn't even surprise me. It was too easy to conform. I had no anchor or grounding in the faith.

The Christian life is about imitating Christ. We are to grow in Christlikeness the longer we walk with Him. That means we are laying down our lives, our wants, and our aspirations, and we are to follow Him (as we highlighted in an earlier chapter). This roots and anchors us to a solid foundation, and it allows us to grow and mature in our faith. If we have that foundation and truly live to imitate Christ, it will be difficult to conform to the culture.

People are like trees. The roots in our lives determine the fruits of our lives. Where our roots are planted will shape the fruits that spring from us. If our roots are in people-pleasing, acceptance, and being liked, then the fruit of our lives will be conformity to whatever secures those things. If our roots are in obeying God, denying self, and surrendering to Scripture, then our fruits will be faithfulness, perseverance, and transformation.

TRANSFORMED

Paul says in Romans 12:2, "Do not be conformed to this world, but be transformed by the renewal of your mind, that by testing you may discern what is the will of God, what is good and acceptable and perfect." Instead of conforming to the world, believers are transformed by the renewal of our minds. Only believers with renewed minds can discern the will of God. A transformed mind can know what God desires and wants from our lives.

Another byproduct of a transformed mind is the ability to discern what is good, acceptable, and perfect to God. This corresponds with knowing God's will. Believers must resist letting the world conform us into its image. We must rely upon God to help us know the truth with clarity. Fortunately, there is no need to guess about God-glorifying ethics and morals. Through His Word, we know what God says is good and acceptable.

The world preaches that homosexuality is good. It treats transgenderism as acceptable. How do we discern if the world has it right or wrong? We need our minds transformed to understand what God thinks. God's Word must usurp the will of the culture and our flesh. The will of God alone is good, acceptable, and perfect. We need minds capable of observing cultural truth claims about morality and discerning whether it aligns with God's will.

Most actors, athletes, and music artists serve as evangelists for the culture's ever-shifting morality. They are the lead disciple-makers of cultural orthodoxy. But Christians do not take our cues from outside of Scripture. We look to God's Word to shape our minds and understanding. The rest of this chapter highlights areas where Christians today need transformed minds.

AN ETERNAL PERSPECTIVE

One struggle in our battle against conforming to the world is forgetting eternity. This life is not the end of the story. Jesus showed us this in the Luke 9 passage we saw in a previous chapter. There's no victory in gaining the world but losing your soul. It is a losing exchange to win the world's favor and approval if you forfeit God's.

People exchange acceptance from God for the approval of man when they lose sight of eternity. We forget that those who live in sin and rebellion will not escape His judgment. Those who mock, oppress, and deny the truth of God will one day stand before Him. When we feel the pressure to conform around us, our minds must lay hold of this truth.

In Psalm 73, Asaph talks about his struggle with what he witnessed around him. He thought those who loved and obeyed God were struggling, and those who rejected God's ways were thriving. What was the point of living holy if the wicked prospered and the righteous suffered? Why did he keep his heart clean when rebellion against God seemed to go unpunished and undeterred? These things bothered him deeply. He almost fell away from the faith. He almost walked away from God. But then something changed. What brought him back?

Asaph says in Psalm 73:16-17, "But when I thought how to understand this, it seemed to me a wearisome task, until I went into the sanctuary of God; then I discerned their end." When Asaph sought God, he came to recognize the deadly end of those who live in rebellion. This brought his heart to rest. He realized these seemingly prosperous people were not living in freedom. They were slaves to sin. These folks were not enjoying a consequence free life. They were storing up wrath that God would release when they stood before Him.

Only when Asaph had an eternal perspective did he see and understand the effects and consequences of sin and rebellion. Once he recognized that judgment awaited the unrighteous people around him, he could resist his desire to join them and continue to pursue righteousness.

We need this reminder too. The moral landscape today rejoices in wrongdoing and lies. People malign the truth and attack it daily. Meanwhile, sin is celebrated and called beautiful, good, and true. Our world rebels against God, His Word, and His ways. And often it looks as if there are no consequences for this. Christians are called bigots, racists, homophobes, and transphobes for not going along with the culture's dogmas. It makes conforming desirable.

We need to let God's Word give us an eternal focus so we don't forget that God will ultimately judge the words, actions, and ideas of all men. Being on "the right side of history" is a slogan people toss around to entice or coerce others to jump on board with the world's thoughts and values. But as Christians, we know that being on the right side of history means siding with what God says, because God is the one who will assess history as its righteous Judge.

OUR TRUE AUTHORITY

It's popular for churchgoing people to affirm the Bible is God's Word. We can check all the boxes about Scripture being true, without error, and the source of where we know God. But many who affirm these truths in word don't practice them in deed. Many say the Bible is God's Word, but do not live with the Bible as their ultimate authority.

This is an easy trap for professing Christians to fall into. When at church, we "amen" all the doctrinal statements, but when we leave church and go back to our "regular lives" our Bibles don't play much of a role in how we think and live. We need a transformation to occur. We need to place the Bible in its proper place in our lives as the true authority, and not affirm it in name only. The Scriptures must become our true authority, not just our theoretical authority.

The Bible becomes a theoretical authority when we say we believe it to be God's Word, but we don't let it shape our understanding of sexuality, gender, forgiveness, salvation, or any other subject. If we let what the world says about sexuality and gender determine our ethics, instead of the Bible, then the Scriptures are not our true authority. The world is. When the culture shapes our understanding of gender more than Scripture, the Bible isn't our true authority. We need our minds transformed by placing Scripture as the true authority over our thinking.

An illustration may help communicate the problem we face in the church today. Imagine for a moment that I'm with a friend, and that friend tries to open a door that's locked. He fidgets with it for a moment and gives up. But then I tell him, "Hey, don't worry, I have the key." Imagine if I approached the door to unlock it and my friend said, "Oh, no no, I don't believe in keys." If I were to hear that statement, and then put the key back in my pocket and walk away from the door, what should you conclude?

Answer this question: In that scenario, which one of us didn't believe in keys, me or my friend? You could say my friend didn't believe in keys because he said he didn't. But—follow me closely here—you could also conclude I didn't believe in keys either. Why? Because instead of showing him that the key opened the door, I showed my unbelief in keys by putting it back in my pocket and walking away.

What's the point of the illustration? The world is looking for answers, grasping for solutions to problems, and reaching for understanding. And Christians have an answer. We have *the* answer. We have the key that unlocks the door.

The Word of God, given to us, reveals the nature and will of God, and shows us who we are and what we need most. But when many Christians attempt to bring the Bible into the conversation, the world says, "We don't believe in the Bible." And instead of stepping forward with conviction about how the Bible speaks to these things, we back away and put our Bibles aside. Why? Because many of us don't believe in the Bible either. Too many professing Christians say they believe the Bible but hold only a theoretical belief. Sadly, the Bible is often not the true authority of professing believers.

That must change.

The transformed mind we need requires that the Bible take its rightful place as our authority. The Bible tells us how we should think and live. It's time for Christians to be Bible people again. If we are going to stand firm as Christians in a changing world, and if we're going to avoid the allure of conforming to the culture, then we must let the Scriptures transform our minds to know God's will. We must develop an eternal perspective on life and not live only for the moment. And the Scriptures must become our actual authority, and not our authority in name only.

Armed with these things, we can choose to live for Christ in this world. And that is the subject of our last chapter.

Discussion Questions

1. Why do you think many people abandon God's Word as being authoritative in their lives?

2. What is our ultimate source to determine right or wrong, regardless of what the culture might say?

3. Why are we drawn to acceptance in this world vs. having an eternal perspective?

4. In what areas of your life do you need to bring your actions in alignment with your doctrine? What must you set aside to recognize the Bible's authority in your life?

5. List some Bible verses below that will encourage you in seeking to be transformed by Christ.

7

LIVING WITH BOLDNESS

I don't envy the younger generations. It is hard for anybody to be a faithful Christian in this culture, but it's especially tough for younger people. Rejection hurts. Fear of it drives our decisions and choices. All of us crave the approval of our peers. And as our culture moves further and further out of alignment with Christian beliefs, the pressure to conform will only grow.

But we must resist it. We must fight the urge to blend in with the crowds. Faithfulness honors God, submits to Him, and declares His ways, even when the world rejects or hates us for it. Living this way requires boldness.

Boldness is courage and conviction in action. It isn't brashness or rudeness—though people often excuse those behaviors by claiming they're just "being bold." Too many professing Christians act like jerks, particularly on social media, in the name of boldness.

I've done this before. But the truth is, we must not deceive ourselves into thinking quarrelsomeness, crudeness, slander, or contentiousness are ever justified, not even in the name of "fighting for truth." Our zeal for truth cannot become an occasion for sin. We must always maintain Christian character in our bold defense and proclamation of the truth.

Real boldness, biblical boldness, is action fueled by our beliefs and lived out with courage. It requires boldness to be a faithful Christian in today's culture. But we are not simply contrarians. Our goal is to be found faithful, not to "own the libs" or rack up followers. To stand against the headwinds of culture, we need strong Christian convictions and strong Christian character.

Don't miss this: Conformity is inevitable when we hold loose convictions. It takes true courage to live against the grain of our culture. We must be prepared to lose approval, popularity, and comfort. That takes courage.

RISKY BUSINESS

One of the great New Testament models of courage is John the Baptist. John shows up on the scene as a man that did not fit the mold of the people around him. He dressed weird. He ate bugs. He lived in the wilderness. But most importantly, he spoke with authority on the things of God and did not care about people's opinions of him.

When the Pharisees heard that many people were going out to be baptized by John, they went to see what was happening for themselves (Matthew 3:7-11). When John saw them approaching, he called them out in front of the crowds. He expected their dismissal of his baptism. He knew they thought it was unnecessary for them as Jews. That was something God-fearing Gentiles did for acceptance from YHWH, not the children of Abraham. The Pharisees believed their privileged status as children of Abraham exempted them from needing to repent and ready their hearts for the coming Messiah. But John didn't mind confronting them head-on with the truth.

He did not tiptoe around political leaders either. John called out Herod Antipas (the Roman-backed ruler of Galilee) for divorcing his wife and marrying his brother's wife, Herodias (Matthew 13:1-14). John spoke boldly against this sin. This led to his eventual arrest and death by beheading.

The forerunner of the Messiah gave his life in service to the truth. His boldness is an example for every Christian. His death is too. Standing for the truth of God in a world that despises it is costly. It always has been, and it always will be.

OUR HERITAGE

The book of Acts is one of the most exciting books in the entire Bible. We watch as the resurrected Jesus ascends to Heaven and commands His disciples to make more disciples in all the world. In Acts 2, the Holy Spirit falls upon the believers gathered in Jerusalem, and Peter preaches a sermon that three thousand people respond to with faith and baptism. This scene depicts the birth of the Church in Acts. And today the church carries on that mission to make disciples by reaching the lost, baptizing them, and building up the local church.

As we look at the early believers, living out their faith and obeying Jesus' commands, the prevailing theme is boldness. The book of Acts captures this throughout its pages. Read the passages I reference below with precision and notice the predominance of boldness.

Now when they saw the boldness of Peter and John, and perceived that they were uneducated, common men, they were astonished. And they recognized that they had been with Jesus. — Acts 4:13

Peter and John's demeanor and manner of speaking displayed boldness to every observer. They didn't have advanced degrees or a respectable family pedigree. They were common men who had walked with Jesus. But their convictions and courage produced a visible boldness.

Later, after an angel rescued Peter and John from jail, they met with the church in Jerusalem. They rejoiced together and then prayed:

And now, Lord, look upon their threats and grant to your servants to continue to speak your word with all boldness, while you stretch out your hand to heal, and signs and wonders are performed through the name of your holy servant Jesus." And when they had prayed, the place in which they were gathered together was shaken, and they were all filled with the Holy Spirit and continued to speak the word of God with boldness. — Acts 4:29-31

They asked for boldness, and the Spirit continued fueling them to speak the Word of God with boldness. This led to their second arrest. This time the religious leaders roughed them up and let them go, warning them to quit preaching Christ:

and when they had called in the apostles, they beat them and charged them not to speak in the name of Jesus, and let them go. Then they left the presence of the council, rejoicing that they were counted worthy to suffer dishonor for the name. And every day, in the temple and from house to house, they did not cease teaching and preaching that the Christ is Jesus. — Acts 5:40-42

How many of us, after being arrested, beaten, and warned to stop preaching Christ, would continue on? They did. They rejoiced that Jesus counted them worthy to suffer for His name. They basically slapped high-fives on the way out, shocked that Jesus let them take beatings in His name. Can you imagine it?

Picture John looking at Peter, "Man, they bopped you pretty good on that eye. It's swelling shut!"

Imagine Peter laughing as he replies, "I know, right? Isn't it awesome?"

We can't fathom this kind of response today because we lack their boldness. Not only would we go whining back to our homes, griping because Jesus didn't protect us from the thrashing we just received, but most of us would never say anything else that could lead to another beating.

Think about it and ask yourself: How would you respond? Would you rejoice that Jesus counted you worthy to suffer for His name? Would you resolve to keep sharing the gospel with others no matter what it cost? Reflect on that for a minute.

Your answer matters. For a growing number of believers today, a response to persecution is likely to be more than hypothetical. Boldness is essential for faithfulness.

Paul and Barnabas went into Gentile country and gathered both Jews and Gentiles together to preach to them. When the Jews rejected the gospel in that area, they responded:

And Paul and Barnabas spoke out boldly, saying, "It was necessary that the word of God be spoken first to you. Since you thrust it aside and judge yourselves unworthy of eternal life, behold, we are turning to the Gentiles." — Acts 13:46

Paul and Barnabas spoke with boldness. When the Jews in the city rejected them, they didn't quit or pout over their opposition. They decided to take the gospel to the Gentiles. They traveled to new territories to proclaim the name of Christ.

So they remained for a long time, speaking boldly for the Lord, who bore witness to the word of his grace, granting signs and wonders to be done by their hands. — Acts 14:3

As they preached to Jews and Gentiles, many came to faith (Acts 14:1). Even Apollos, a brand-new Christian, started preaching to others. And what marked his speech?

He began to speak boldly in the synagogue, but when Priscilla and Aquila heard him, they took him aside and explained to him the way of God more accurately. — Acts 18:26

In Acts 19, Paul preached in Ephesus to people, confronting their idolatry and false worship. He proclaimed Jesus to them, causing a riot in the city. What kind of preaching produces riots in the city? Bold, persuasive reasoning:

And he entered the synagogue and for three months spoke boldly, reasoning and persuading them about the kingdom of God. — Acts 19:8

Paul stood before King Agrippa and testified to the death and resurrection of Jesus. He then shared his own story of conversion. Paul confronted the king, asking him if he believes these things:

For the king knows about these things, and to him I speak boldly. For I am persuaded that none of these things has escaped his notice, for this has not been done in a corner. — Acts 26:26

Agrippa can't believe Paul is trying to convert him, and in such a short amount of time. But Paul doesn't care, he just wants to see him saved. Boldness.

Lastly, we see Paul in Rome, under house arrest, and what is happening during that time? Is he sulking or whining that he's in this situation? No. The last verse in the book shows us how he lived:

proclaiming the kingdom of God and teaching about the Lord Jesus Christ with all boldness and without hindrance. — Acts 28:31

Boldness. That's the recurring theme of the book of Acts. Have you ever noticed that before? Disciples of Jesus live out their faith with boldness. Their convictions and courage produce faithfulness to Christ in a culture of opposition and hostility. The same must mark our lives.

MORE ON BOLDNESS

As we consider the testimony of Acts, and as we consider what we've covered in this book, we recognize our need for boldness. If we are going to resist conformity, especially in the midst of a culture that does not celebrate Christian beliefs, we must become bold men and women of faith. If we are to stand against the tide, boldness must become a central attribute of the Christian life.

Our culture is growing more godless. The world is broken and in desperate need of the gospel of Jesus. People need to know that God has spoken. They need to hear that the Word of God reveals who God is, who we are, and what God expects of us. In other words, they need us to bear witness to the truth of Scripture.

It is in the Bible that we learn God sent His Son to die for our sins and that He rose from the dead on the third day. The Scriptures teach that eternal life is available to all who repent of their sins and trust Christ. And the Scriptures instruct us about what it means to follow Jesus and live as His disciples. We must boldly proclaim these truths to a world in need.

Paul lived as a bold witness for others to see. As he lived out his faith, it encouraged others to do the same.

And most of the brothers, having become confident in the Lord by my imprisonment, are much more bold to speak the word without fear. — Philippians 1:14

Paul's sufferings for the gospel empowered other believers to share their faith without fear. Their boldness grew through Paul's example. Boldness is contagious. When we see others willing to take heat for their convictions, willing to stand for the truth against the lies of the world, we grow courageous. Something rises in us to live like that. Perhaps you are the individual who creates that spark in others. Maybe your boldness would spur others on to live obediently to Jesus.

Boldness requires dying to self. If we are to live

with conviction, courage, and urgency for Christ, it can't be about us. We cannot maintain a "big deal" mentality or a need for approval and live with a bold witness. Boldness demands we sacrifice our concerns about what others think of us for following Jesus. And this isn't limited to our fears about losing people's approval or even compromising the gospel. It also includes sacrificing our prideful boldness that just wants to win arguments or slam dunk on people. Biblical boldness stands firm for Christ's sake, not for our own.

The Holy Spirit produces boldness in us. We are not mustering up boldness through pep talks or fleshly strength. We need the Holy Spirit to fuel our convictions and courage. Let's pray for it. Let's ask the Lord to grant us boldness, like the believers in the book of Acts. If the Spirit empowers our boldness, then we can follow Jesus and obey God's Word, regardless of what new or daunting challenges and obstacles lie ahead. Spirit-empowered boldness leads us to a dependence upon God through communion with Christ each day. We abide in Jesus and pursue Him.

NEED OF THE HOUR

Our world is in desperate need. It is a need most people are not even aware of. Lost people need Christian men and women, boys and girls, to speak the truth in a world of lies. The culture feeds people a parade of lies and half-truths about sexuality, gender, human origins, human value and worth, and a myriad of other issues.

The world perverts God's beautiful design for sex to be experienced in a marriage covenant between a man and a woman. It normalizes homosexuality. It views polyamory as a valid expression of romantic love. Divorce no longer registers with people as unbiblical. Waiting until marriage before having sex is as foreign as a Martian playing college football. And with transgender ideology taking root, the sexual revolution now aims to normalize pedophilia. But make no mistake, this runaway train of unbridled sexual expression leaves a wreckage of bodies and souls in its wake. Christians must proclaim the beauties and wisdom of God's good design for sexuality. The world needs it.

The world has replaced the simplicity of being born a male or a female with a tsunami of lies about gender fluidity. People are now told their bodies do not tell the truth about who they really are. Gender dysphoria—which can be a genuine experience—is immediately diagnosed in anyone who feels a little uncomfortable in his or her skin or doesn't fit neatly into man-made gender stereotypes.

The truth is God formed us in the womb (Psalm 139:13-16) with intentionality, purpose, and wisdom. God has good plans for us. We are fearfully and wonderfully made. Our genders are not an accident. Christians need to meet the confusion of the moment with biblical truth. We must help people discover God's good and wise creational design of human beings as male and female. We will never flourish while denying the Designer's blueprint for how He made them.

DON'T LIE

Rod Dreher wrote a book called *Live Not By Lies*.[8] In the book, he chronicles the lives of Christians in the Soviet Bloc under the rule of communist Russia during the Cold War. The Stalin-led USSR imposed harsh and strict policies on the people. One of the Christian leaders implored the people to live according to the Bible. They may have lacked the power to persuade the Russian government or change the culture to follow the way of Jesus, but even under the tyranny of communism they could resolve to follow Jesus and not live by lies.

In our own culture, the same is true. We may not possess the influence to see the culture transformed in our lifetimes. Our country may never embrace biblical ethics, but Christians today can refuse to live by lies.

We can refuse to go along with blatant lies against God's revealed will. Christians won't lie about who is male or female. Believers will not lie about what kind of sexuality brings human flourishing. We will not live as if human babies in the womb are disposable to make life more convenient or cover up our mistakes.

---

[8] Dreher, Rod. Live Not By Lies: A Manual for Christian Dissidents. Sentinel (September 29, 2020)

A parable written by a Danish author in 1837 is as relevant today as it ever was. In the story, a vain emperor gets swindled by two visitors to his city. They pretend to make the most lavish clothes in the world, but they also claim the clothes are invisible to stupid people. The emperor gives them provisions to build facilities to make their clothes, but the looms are empty. Officials come to check on the progress, but they see nothing. But nobody admits they see nothing. They're afraid of being considered fools.

The two men tell the emperor his clothes are ready and strip him naked to dress him in his new attire. But he has nothing on. A procession is set up with the whole town in attendance to see the emperor's new clothes. He walks through the street, proud of his attire. Everyone applauds and celebrates as he strolls the city. But a little child, unaware of all the social etiquette and fear of the king, blurts out that the emperor is naked.

Everyone knew it, but their fear of looking foolish kept them silent. They played along. They lived by lies because everyone else went along. Everyone else said it was normal.

We are living in this reality today. Everywhere we turn, we have people telling us the definitions we have always lived by are outdated and insufficient. Marriage, gender, sexuality, and women's reproductive rights all mean something different today than they did in generations prior. And we are told we must accept it all.

"Celebrate," we are told.

"How brave!" people remind us.

It's time for Christians to say what is happening, "The emperor is naked!" We must refuse to live by lies. This requires boldness, and we need the church of Jesus to rise up if we intend to hold the line.

Discussion Questions

1. Boldness doesn't come without a cost. In what parts of your life do you expect the greatest resistance to you holding the line of faith?

2. How might you encourage other believers with your boldness? Who are people in your life who might be more willing to stand firm through your boldness?

3. What are the lies of the culture you feel pressured to accept, adopt, and ally yourself with?

4. What is your hope in light of the judgment, rejection, and persecution you will face by holding the line of biblical truth? How might others be encouraged by seeing you stand firm?

Epilogue

UNWILLING TO BOW

In the 500s BC, three young men found themselves in a foreign land. They were forced to learn a new language, dress in new clothing, and were given new names. Everything about their lives had changed. They went from living in their homeland, with their own dreams about life, to having everything redefined for them. Their lives would never be the same. These men are most famously known by their Babylonian names: Shadrach, Meshach, and Abednego.

In Babylon, these three Hebrew boys found themselves in a pagan culture. They were no longer in a land where people claimed YHWH as the One True God. No, in Babylon, the king fashioned himself as a god. He erected a statue of himself made of gold, exalting himself for the peoples of Babylon to worship him. This king, Nebuchadnezzar, had even provided accompanying music for this exercise with a command for all who heard the music to bow down toward the statue. Just imagine the images of people in the marketplace, at home, or traveling down the road hearing the music and dropping on their faces. King Nebuchadnezzar not only imagined it, he demanded it.

However, the three Hebrew captives from Israel did not bow. It doesn't take long to stand out in a culture where everyone else reacts like roaches to light when the music turns on. As the masses dropped to their faces, Shadrach, Meshach, and Abednego remained standing. The text doesn't tell us what they did while everyone else bowed, but we know what they weren't doing. Their defiance drew attention. And not the good kind.

Some Babylonians went to King Nebuchadnezzar to complain that the Hebrew boys did not bow while everyone else did. It wasn't only Babylonians bowing down, but those from many nations, peoples, and languages. The Babylonians were the greatest force on earth. As they conquered nations over the years, they shipped many of those people to Babylon. Like the Babylonians, these foreign people knew to bow. They obeyed and followed the king's commands just like the native people. Shadrach, Meshach, and Abednego stood out like neon lights flashing for everyone's attention.

The king summoned the three young men and asked them if it was true that they refused to bow. They confessed it was. Then Nebuchadnezzar gave them a warning that they could right the wrong by bowing at that moment to the sound of the music. His warning included a threat of death by fire. He even scoffed at them and questioned what kind of God could save them from his hand.

The king teased them in this way because their commitment to God kept them from falling to the ground and worshipping him. He couldn't believe they would refuse to bow before the man who had the power to kill them on the spot. Why would these men honor their deity instead of the king threatening to toss them into a fiery furnace?

The boys responded to the king with astonishing words of courage. They said, "If this be so, our God whom we serve can deliver us from the burning fiery furnace, and he will deliver us out of your hand, O king. But if not, let it be known to you, O king, that we will not serve your gods or worship the golden image you have set up" (Daniel 3:17-18). They knew God could save them, but they made no demands that He had to. If necessary, they would go into the furnace, but they would not worship Nebuchadnezzar or bow to his statue.

REFUSAL TO BOW

These three young men, facing threats from the most powerful man in the world, held the line. They refused to bow the knee to Nebuchadnezzar. Everyone else in Babylon bowed down. Of course they did; it was easier than standing. But the example of these three courageous boys exemplifies the courage we need in the church today. Christians can follow the example of Shadrach, Meshach, and Abednego, remembering that our convictions should drive our actions, not what is popular or easy to do.

As our culture continues to bow to everything but Christ, we as believers must remain standing. Others will quickly spot your refusal to bow. It will cost you popularity, comfort, and the approval of the cultural gatekeepers. It may cost you friendships, family relationships, or your career. But we shouldn't place our identity in those things. We want to honor and please God. We want Christ to be magnified in our lives.

Will you be faithful at all costs? Are you willing to believe God can save you from all ridicule for your obedience, yet be willing to receive it for not bowing the knee? May God raise up a people in this world who refuse to bow.

We need men and women, boys and girls, with a heart and passion to honor God and His Word. We need people who will contend for the faith. Each generation must fight the good fight of faith. We must run the race set before us. That means we are not living at this moment by accident, but by the plan of God (Acts 17:26).

What will you do in this culture of conformity, as it tries with all its might to pull you away from orthodox faith and practice? You must engage in the battle. Though the fighting may be fierce, and the war long endures, we know the victory is ours through Jesus.

Pastor Charles Spurgeon tells us, "A church that does not exist to reclaim heathenism, to fight evil, to destroy error, to put down falsehood, a church that does not exist to take the side of the poor, to denounce injustice and to hold up righteousness, is a church that has no right to be. Not for yourself, O church, do you exist, any more than Christ existed for Himself."[9] We are called to hold the line. Will you answer the call?

CHOOSE THIS DAY

This book isn't long, but I pray it challenges you to live differently. We need courageous Christians in our world today. Conformity is a temptation that surrounds us at every step. Being faithful to the Lord in a world that grows increasingly hostile towards him requires us to draw a line in the sand each day.

We find some of the most powerful words in all of Scripture in Deuteronomy 30. Moses is giving his farewell speech to Israel. They are about to enter the land that God promised them. He knows they have divided hearts. They have been in the wilderness for a long time. Often, they longed for the meager provisions they received as slaves in Egypt rather than trusting God to deliver them the Promised Land. After re-

---

[9] C. H. Spurgeon (2004). "Spurgeon's Sermons on the Death and Resurrection of Jesus", p.294, Hendrickson Publishers

stating the covenant God made with Israel, along with the blessings and curses attached to it, Moses then gives a powerful conclusion.

"See, I have set before you today life and good, death and evil. If you obey the commandments of the Lord your God that I command you today, by loving the Lord your God, by walking in his ways, and by keeping his commandments and his statutes and his rules, then you shall live and multiply, and the Lord your God will bless you in the land that you are entering to take possession of it. But if your heart turns away, and you will not hear, but are drawn away to worship other gods and serve them, I declare to you today, that you shall surely perish. You shall not live long in the land that you are going over the Jordan to enter and possess. I call heaven and earth to witness against you today, that I have set before you life and death, blessing and curse. Therefore choose life, that you and your offspring may live, loving the Lord your God, obeying his voice and holding fast to him, for he is your life and length of days, that you may dwell in the land that the Lord swore to your fathers, to Abraham, to Isaac, and to Jacob, to give them." —

Deuteronomy 30:15-20

Moses appeals to Israel, and I conclude this book by appealing to you: Choose life. Love the Lord your God and walk in His ways. That's where you find life. Keep His statutes and commandments, for they breed life and blessing on us. Do not turn your hearts away from Him.

The goodness and kindness of God are part of the reason He is worthy of our undivided worship. Do not let your heart worship the approval of the culture or world around us. The temptation will always be there, but each day the choice is before us. What will you choose? Life or death?

Choose life and live! Walk in the joy of Christ alone. Use your life to bear witness to Him in a dark world. The world is dying, and many who profess to be Christians are choosing death. May we stay the course, with the help of God and other believers. Hold the line!

ACKNOWLEDGMENTS

This book has my name on the cover, but it has been helped by many other sets of hands. I'm thankful for so many different people's assistance and help along the way.

Thank you, John Page. Your leadership and labor for KJM is a large reason why we are seeing the ministry grow. I'm thankful the Lord linked us up in this work.

A special thanks is owed to Terri McAngus, who volunteers her time to this ministry to help edit everything from daily devotions to projects like this. She is the best.

Another debt of gratitude is due to Josh Wester, who served as the content editor for both of my books. Josh is a skilled editor and theological thinker, but even more, he's a friend.

Thank you TJC for your support and encouragement to pursue Knowing Jesus Ministries. You are a joy to pastor. And to the elders and staff of TJC, thank you for letting me pursue projects such as these so that more than just members of TJC can benefit from the glories found in the truth of Scripture.

ABOUT THE AUTHOR

Erik is the Founder and Lead Pastor of The Journey Church (tjclive.com) in Lebanon, TN, a church that exists to show Jesus as incomparably glorious. The Journey Church is committed to making gospel-rich theology accessible to everyday people. The church reaches a diverse range of people, and continues to grow in both numbers and ministry opportunities to make disciples of Jesus.

He also founded Knowing Jesus Ministries (kjmin.org), a non-profit organization which exists to proclaim timeless truth for everyday life. This ministry provides resources for Christians to grow in their daily walk with Jesus, withstand the onslaught of cultural pressures to conform, and prepare Christians for the suffering that comes in this life. Resources include books, daily devotions, articles, theology videos, conferences, nationally televised sermons, and weekend respites for families who have lost children.

He's been married to Katrina since 2002, and has three children: Kaleb (who went to be with the Lord on December 1st, 2019), Kaleigh Grace, and Kyra Piper.